An Artist's JOURNAL

FRANK DI GIACOMO

PUBLISHED BY FIDELI PUBLISHING INC.

ISBN: 978-1-60414-826-8

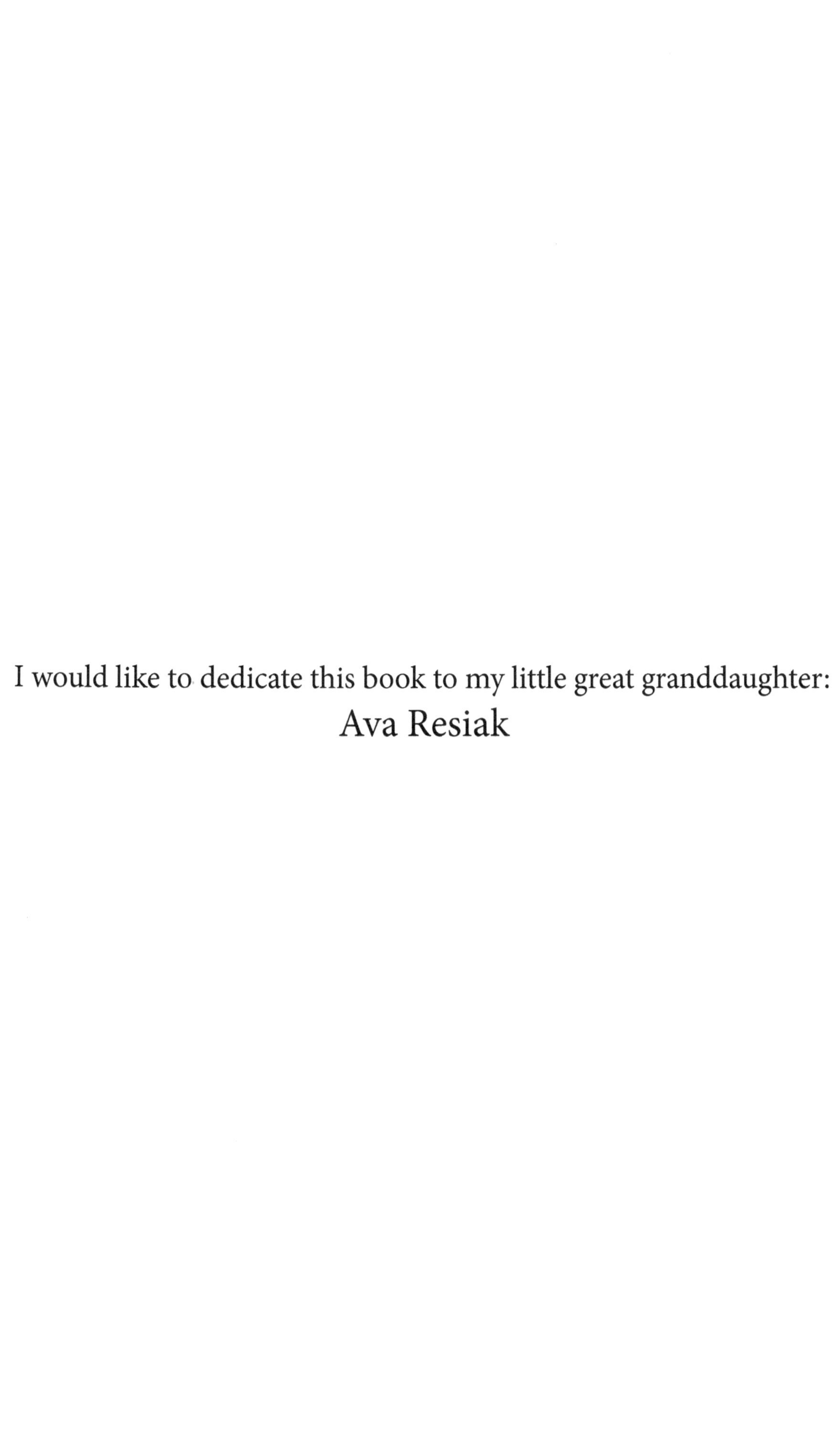

I would like to dedicate this book to my little great granddaughter:
Ava Resiak

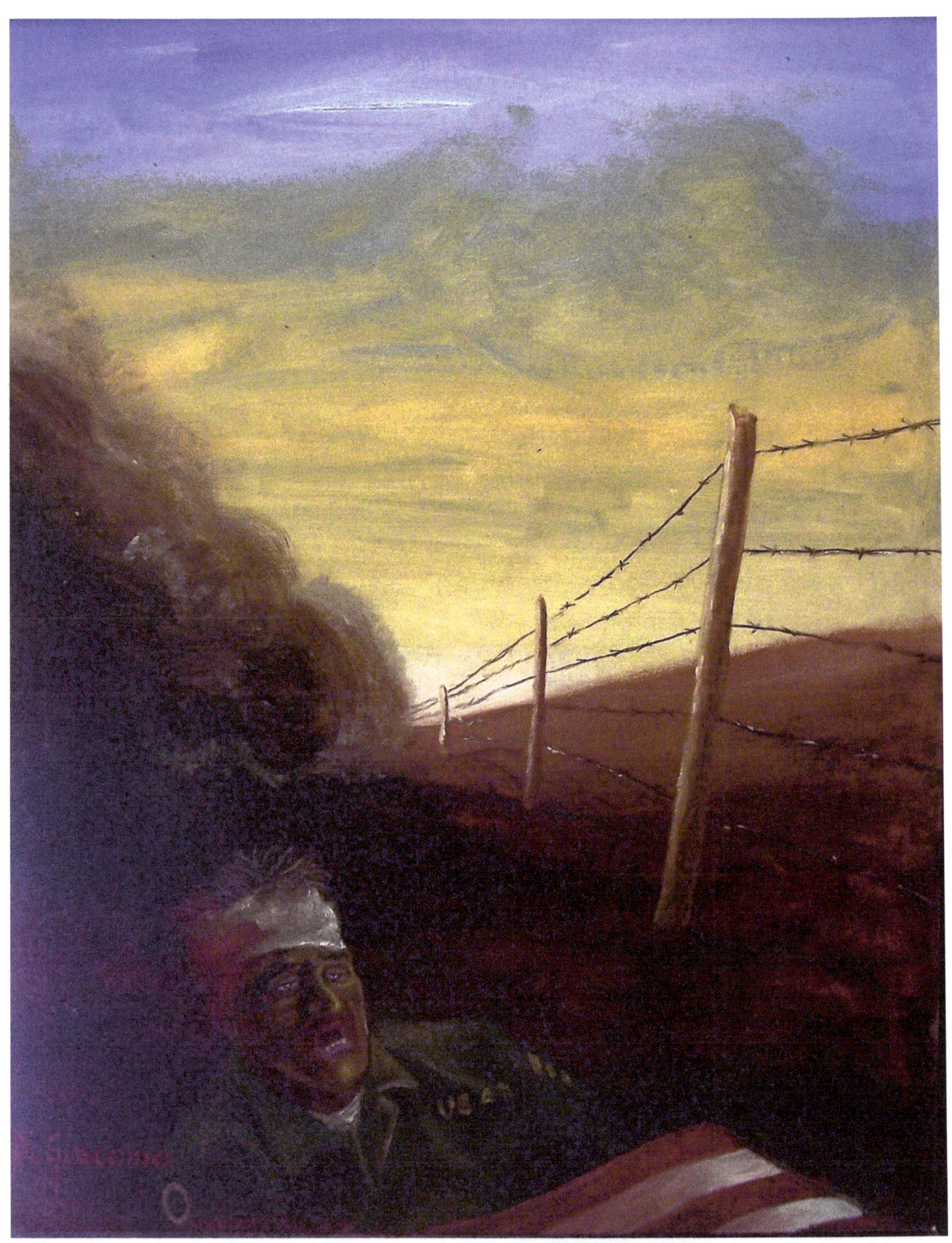

An oil I did and after hearning about the death of Robert Kennedy.

Contents

About this Book and its Author

This journal contains my diary of ideas, hints and suggestions, which led me to reach this level of realistic art that is not taught in any other art book. The proof is illustrated in the following pages and will be referenced throughout this book.

This book was not intended to be a "how to paint for the beginner." It is for the serious person with an artistic soul.

I was born in Ozone Park NY lived there for six years then moved with my parents to Fall River Massachusetts and finally moved here in Michigan City Indiana. All through my school years, I would receive special attention for my art. As an adult I've work as a design engineer and part time as a commercial artist for a local advertising agency. Some of my art work was shown in *Arts and Framing* and other trade magazines.

While in the US Army, I won first place in an art contest and my poster was published in the *Stars and Stripes Newspaper* during my tour in the far east.

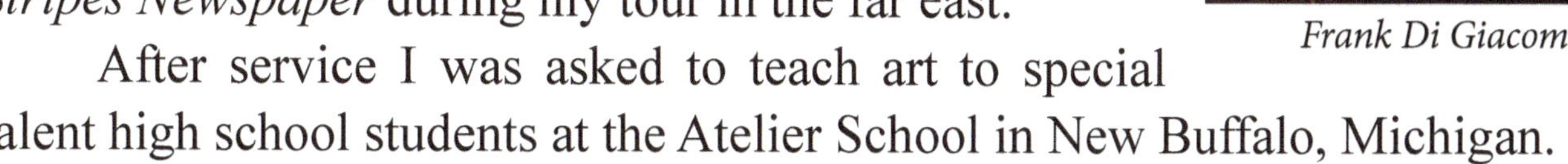

Frank Di Giacomo

After service I was asked to teach art to special talent high school students at the Atelier School in New Buffalo, Michigan.

I have been a member of Michigan City Art League as well as the Chesterton and Southern Shore galleries.

Color

Let's start off with color and how inside and outside atmosphere effects it. For example, if you take two objects that are the same size and color and put one of them close to your eye and the other about 20 feet away, you'll notice the furthest one doesn't look as bright as the one close to you. So, not only is the size effectively smaller but it is less illuminated, as shown in this illustration below. This idea is shown in scenery paintings with a background.

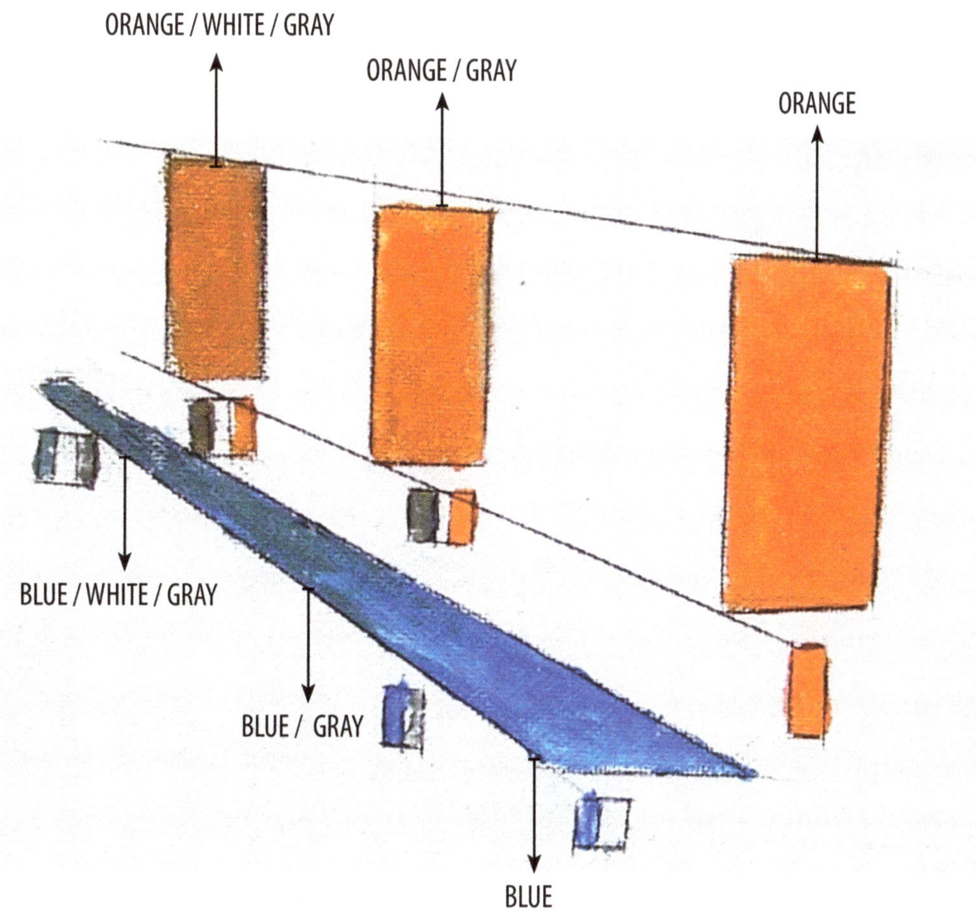

Acrylic Paint

In our last lesson, we learned that atmosphere and distance affect color. With this in mind, the artist must "Grey" his color. This makes you look inside the painting rather than using raw color from the tube, which makes the painting jump out.

Look at the old masters and you will see that the colors are subdued. That is called the van Eyck method after the 15th century painter, Jan van Eyck. They did a monochrome underpaying of a gray tint and then added color, which is great when painting with oils

With acrylics, since acrylics dry faster, you have to premix your paint. Samples of my work on the following pages are oil, acrylic and watercolor. I want to mention that watercolors are an exception, meaning the paints are translucent so when applied, the colors are toned down through absorption by the paper.

Since we are on the subject, when painting shadows be sure they are translucent and muted. A perfect shadow is a mixture of raw umber and ultramarine. A gray and brown mix also can be used with acrylic when applied by brushing lightly. (See illustration on page 3.)

HANDY TIP

LIGHT AND SHADOW

I have added a method that is not true in reality but it is so effective. You can do this by adding a light line to separate the shadow from the resting base. (See illustrations on pages 3-7.) Don't forget to use a soft brush with a light touch over shadow when using oil. Use a stiff brush on acrylic and a soft brush when painting with water.

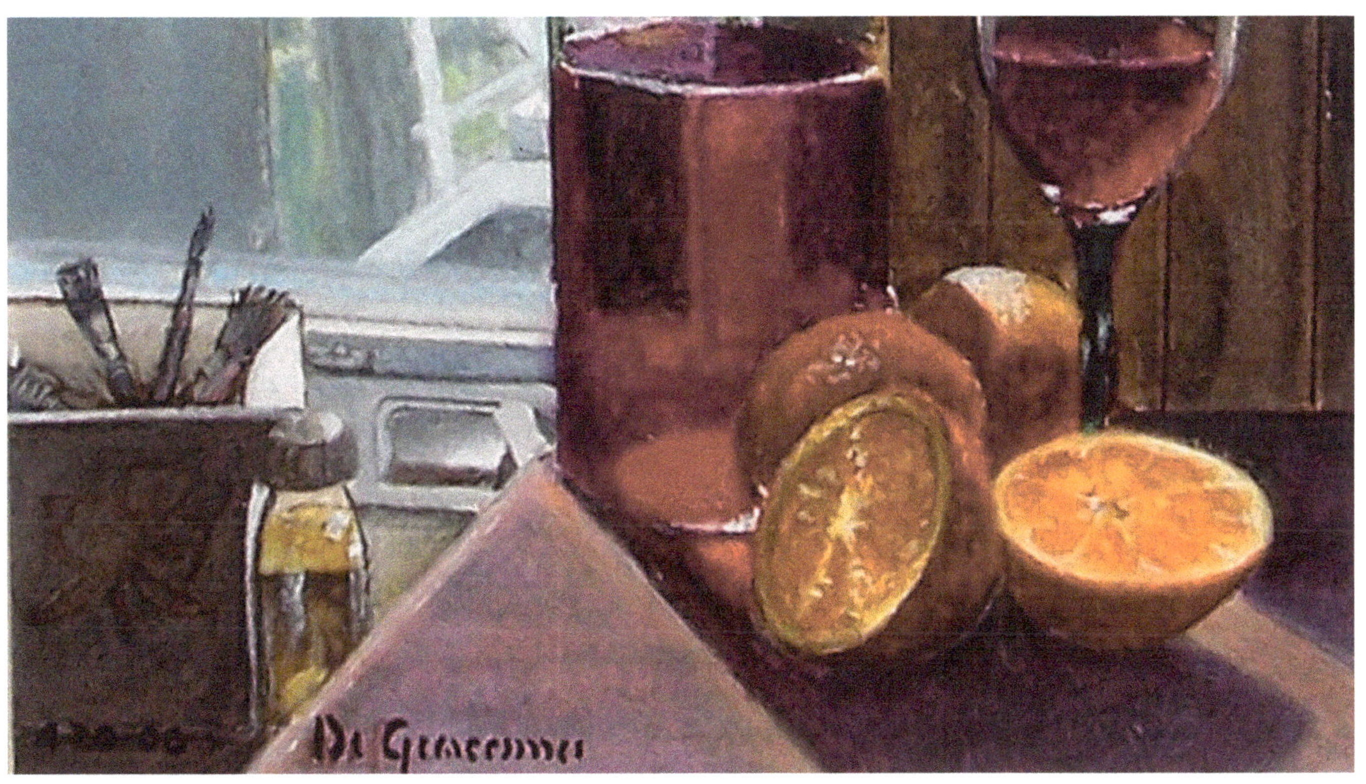

This is a watercolor, note the light line.

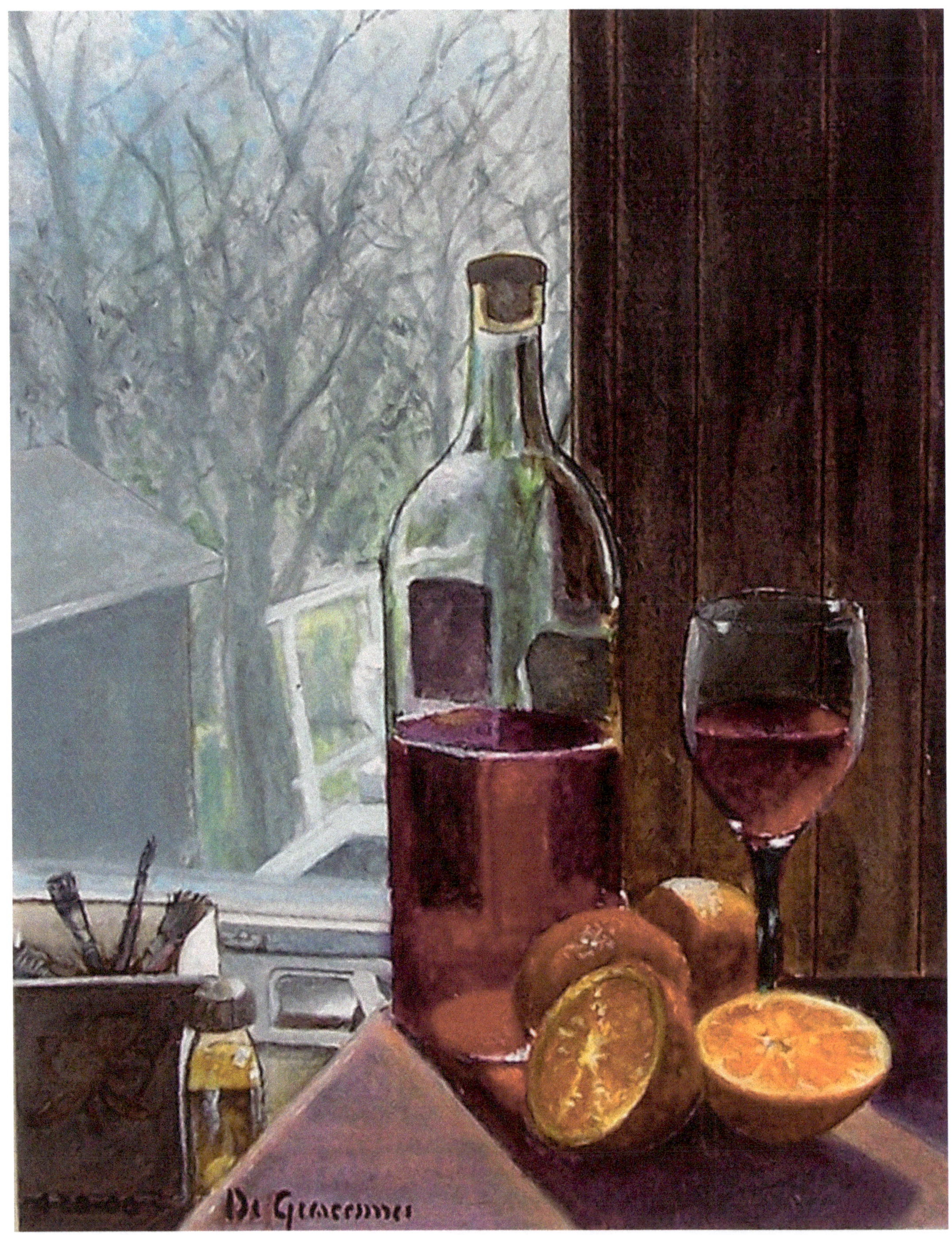

WATER COLOR

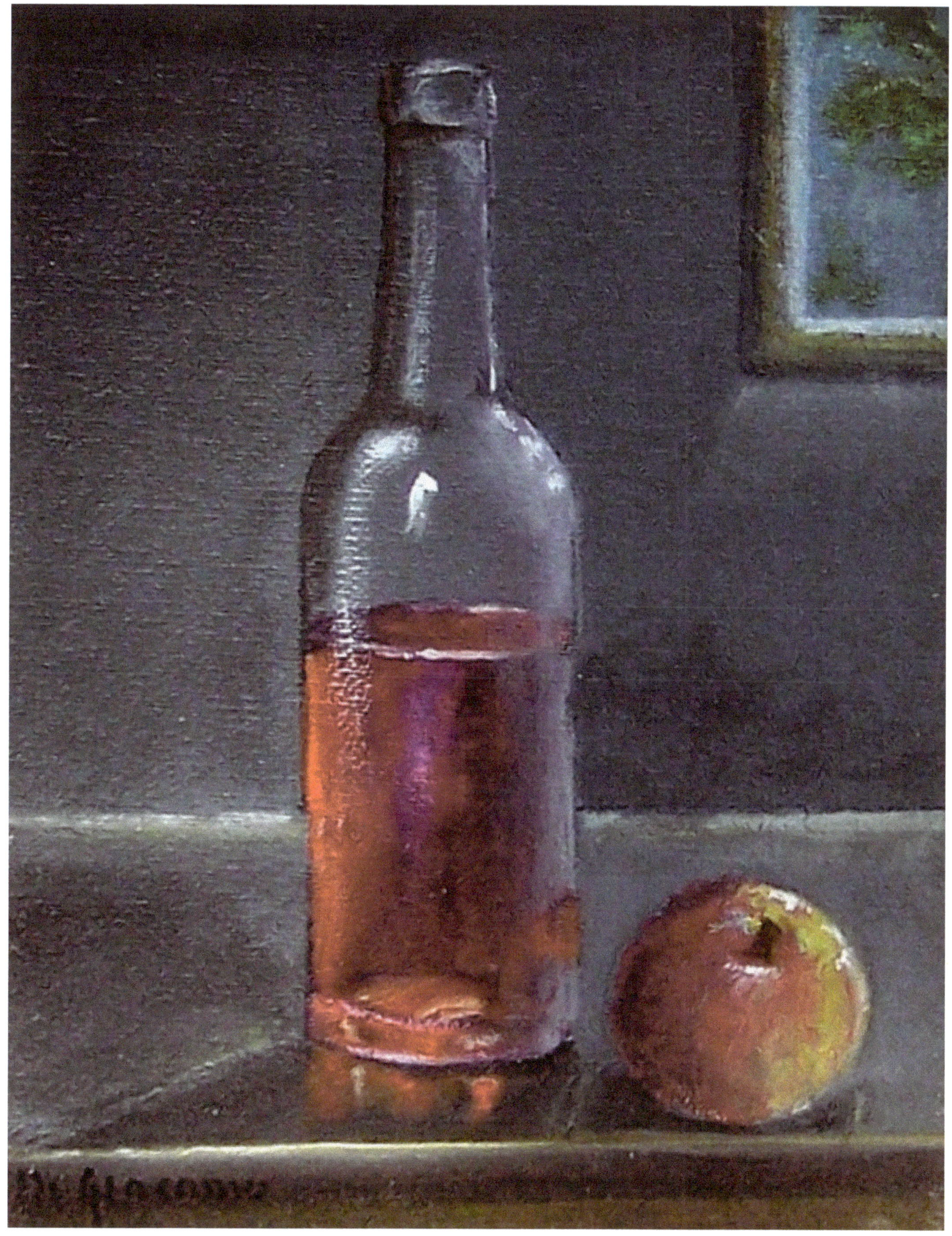

ACRYLIC

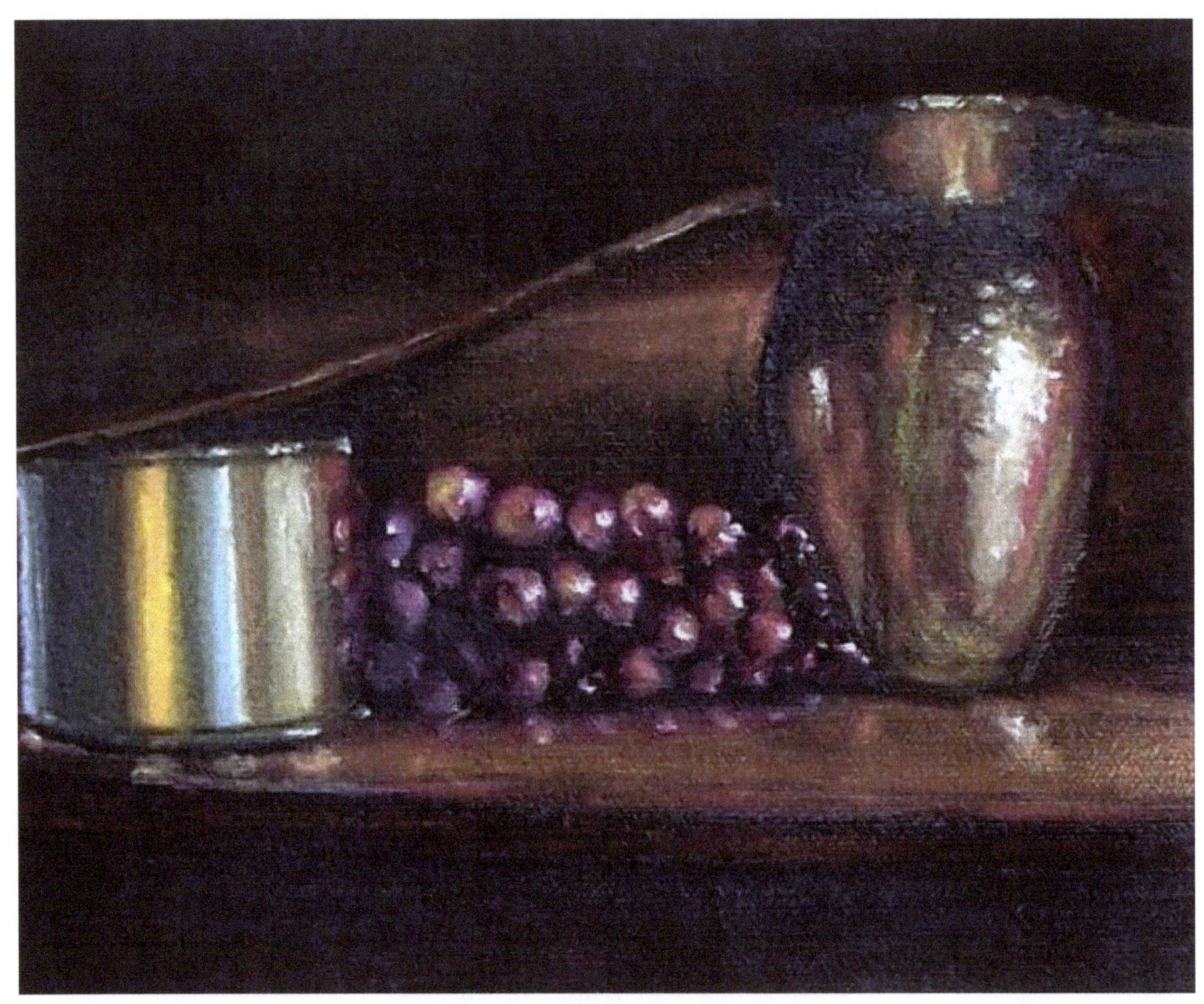

ACRYLIC

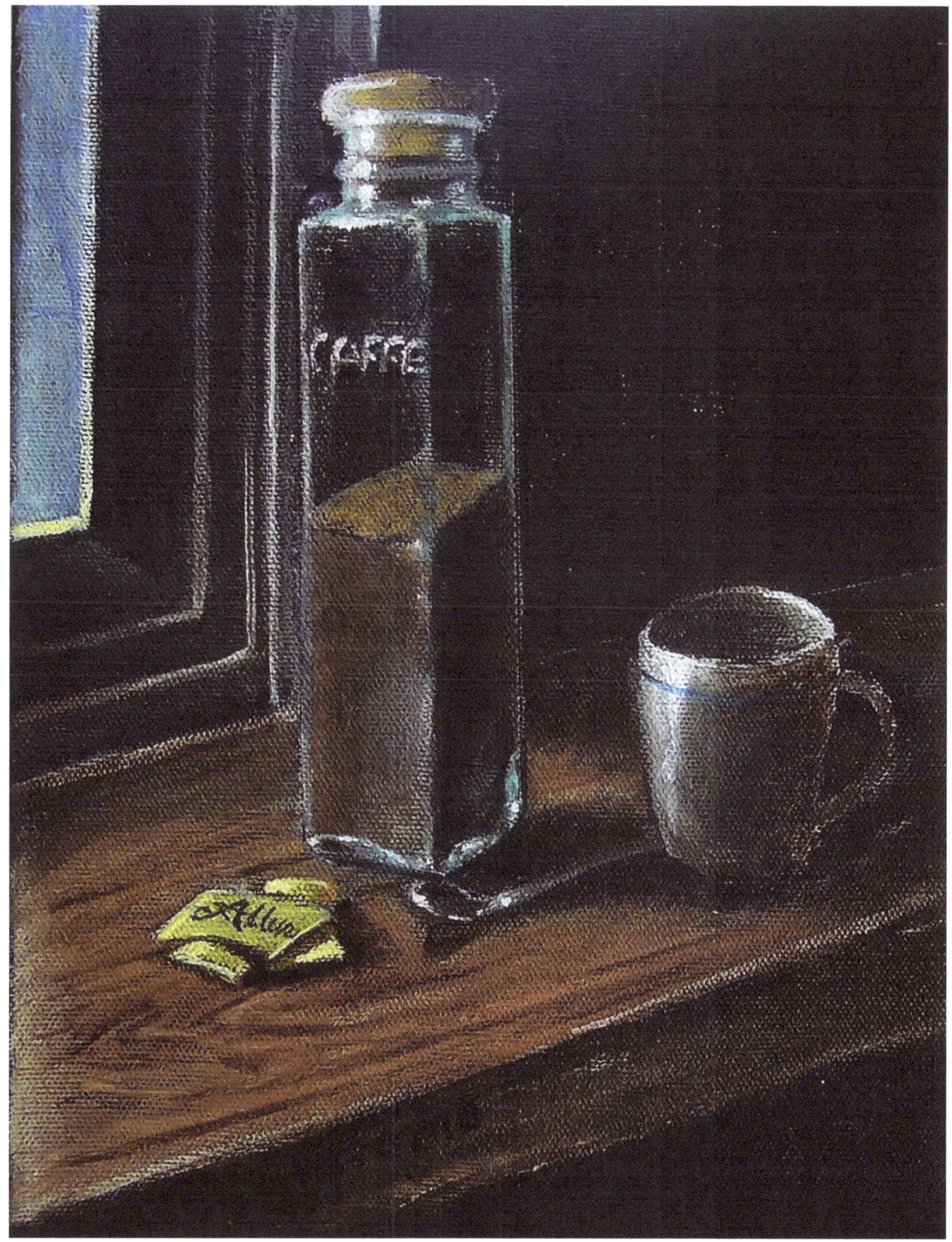

OIL

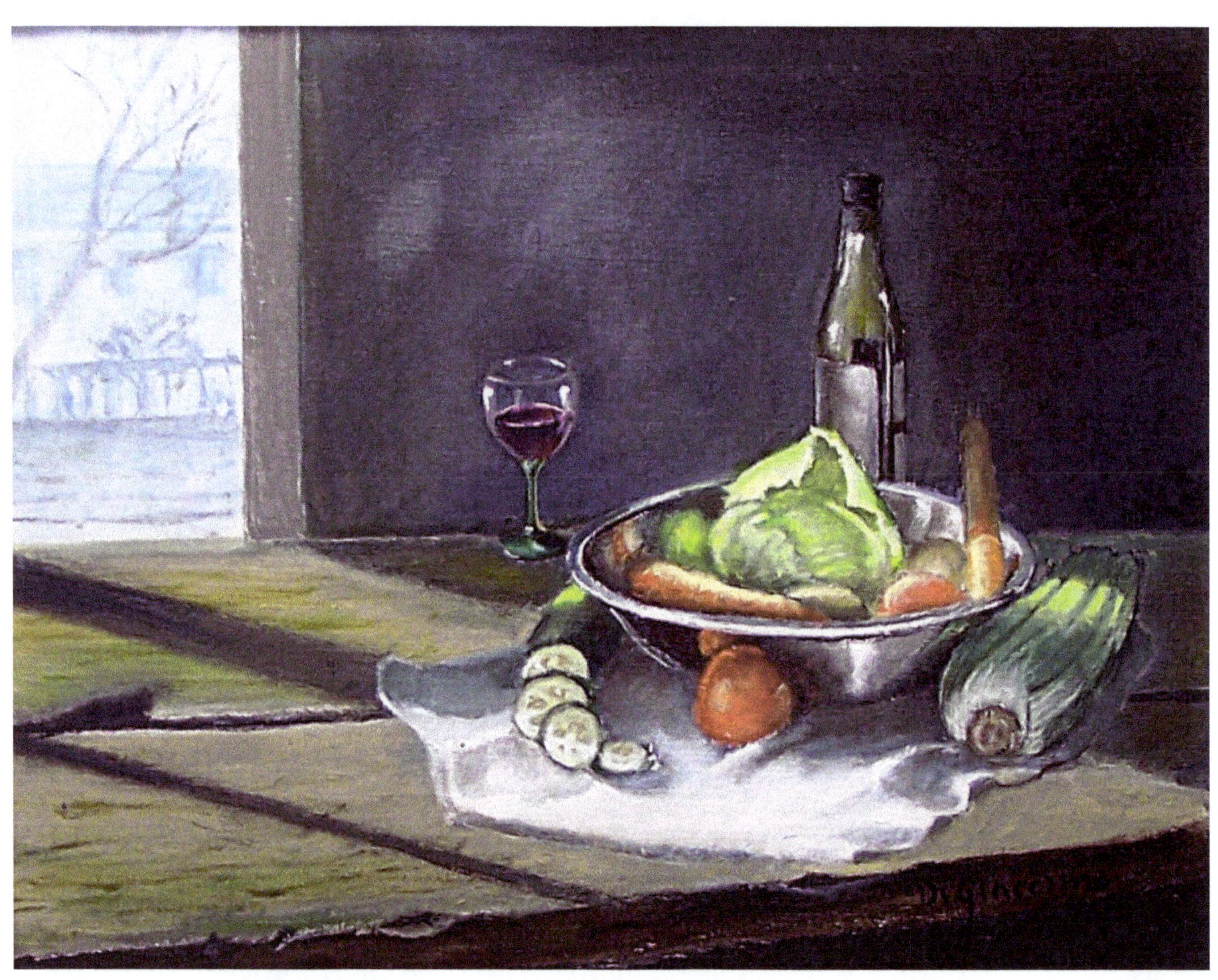

NOTE: The soft shadows here. I should have filled the canva.s — ACRYLIC

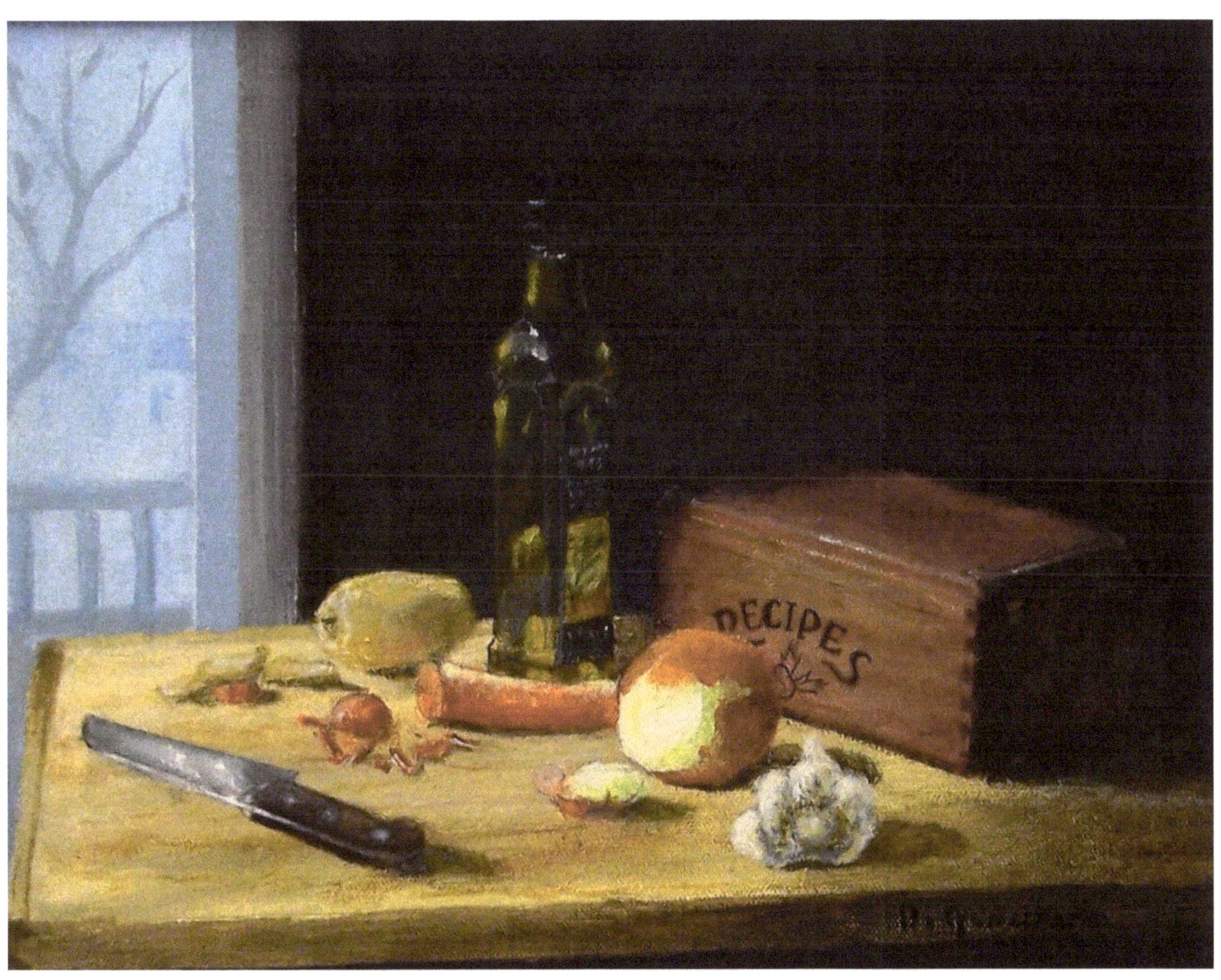

Here I did fill the canvas Note the natural scene. It creates more interest.

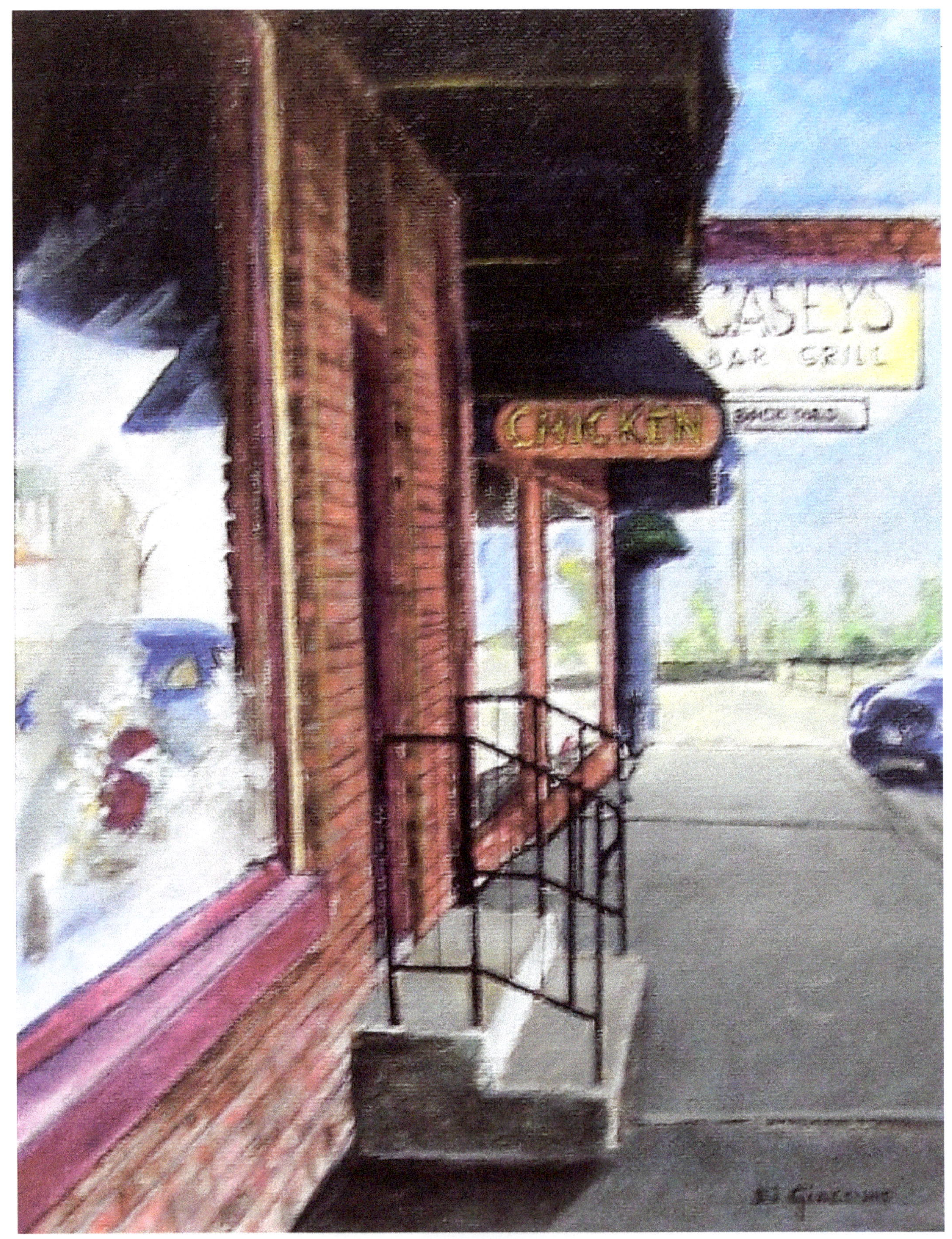

WATERCOLOR

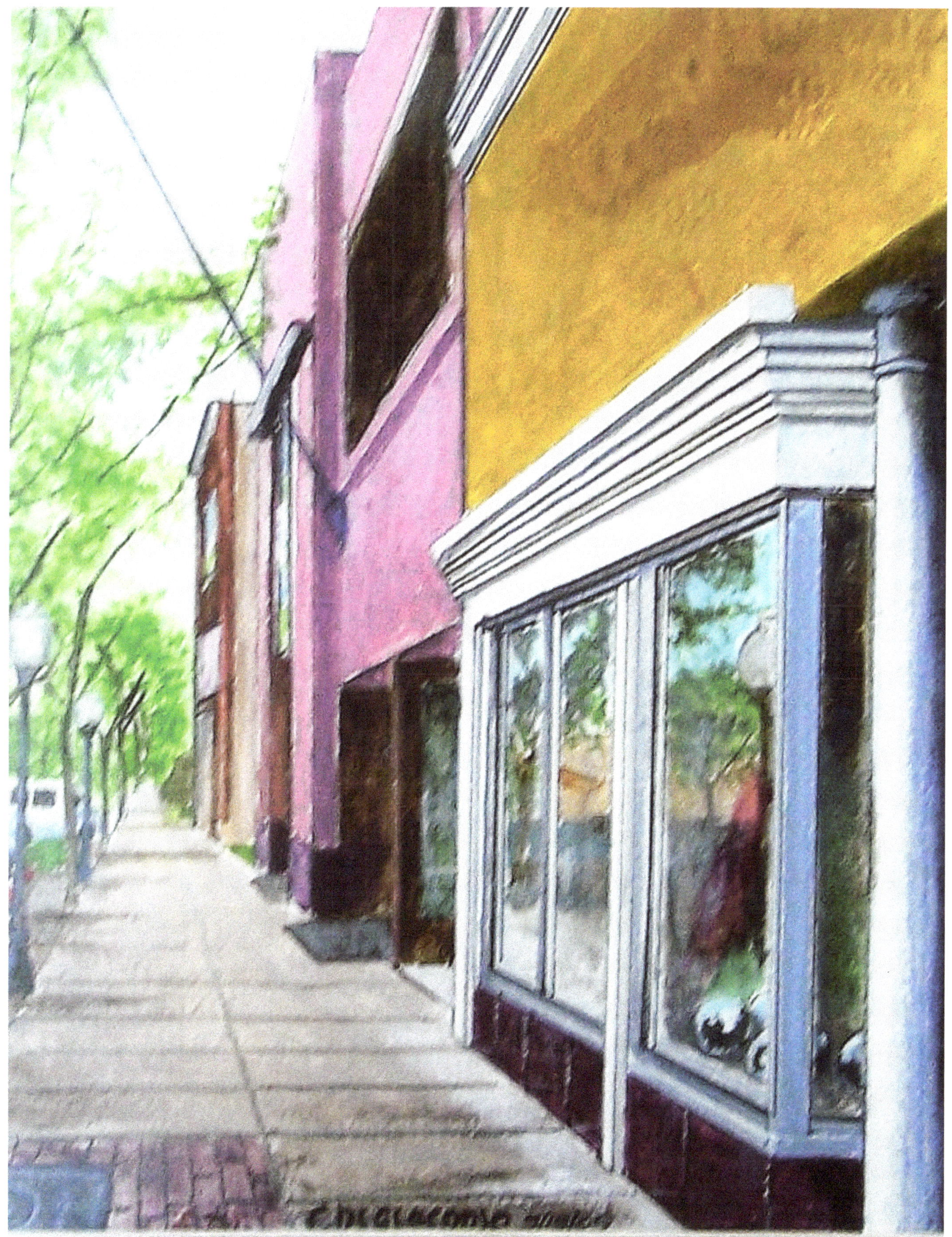

ACRYLIC

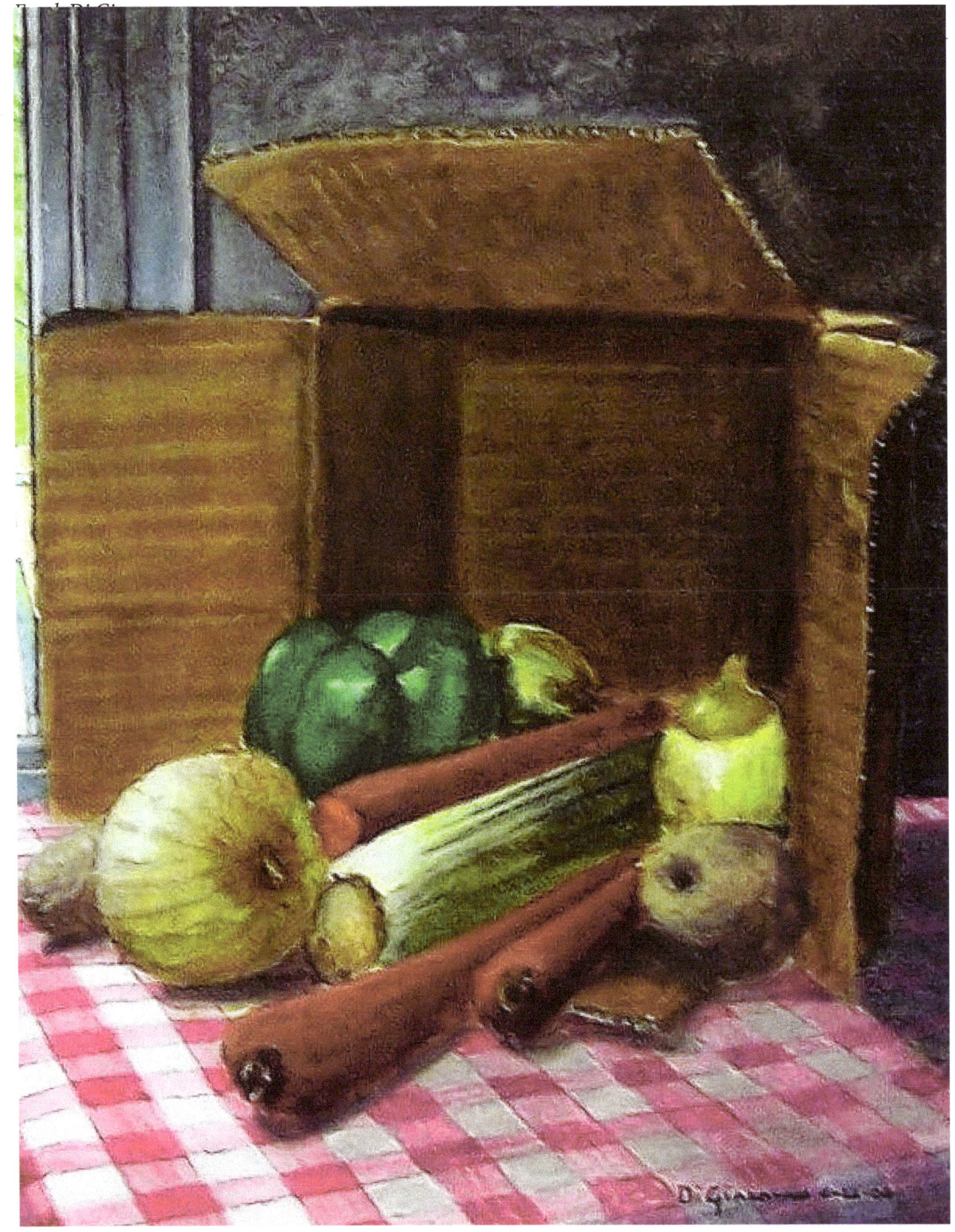

WATERCOLOR

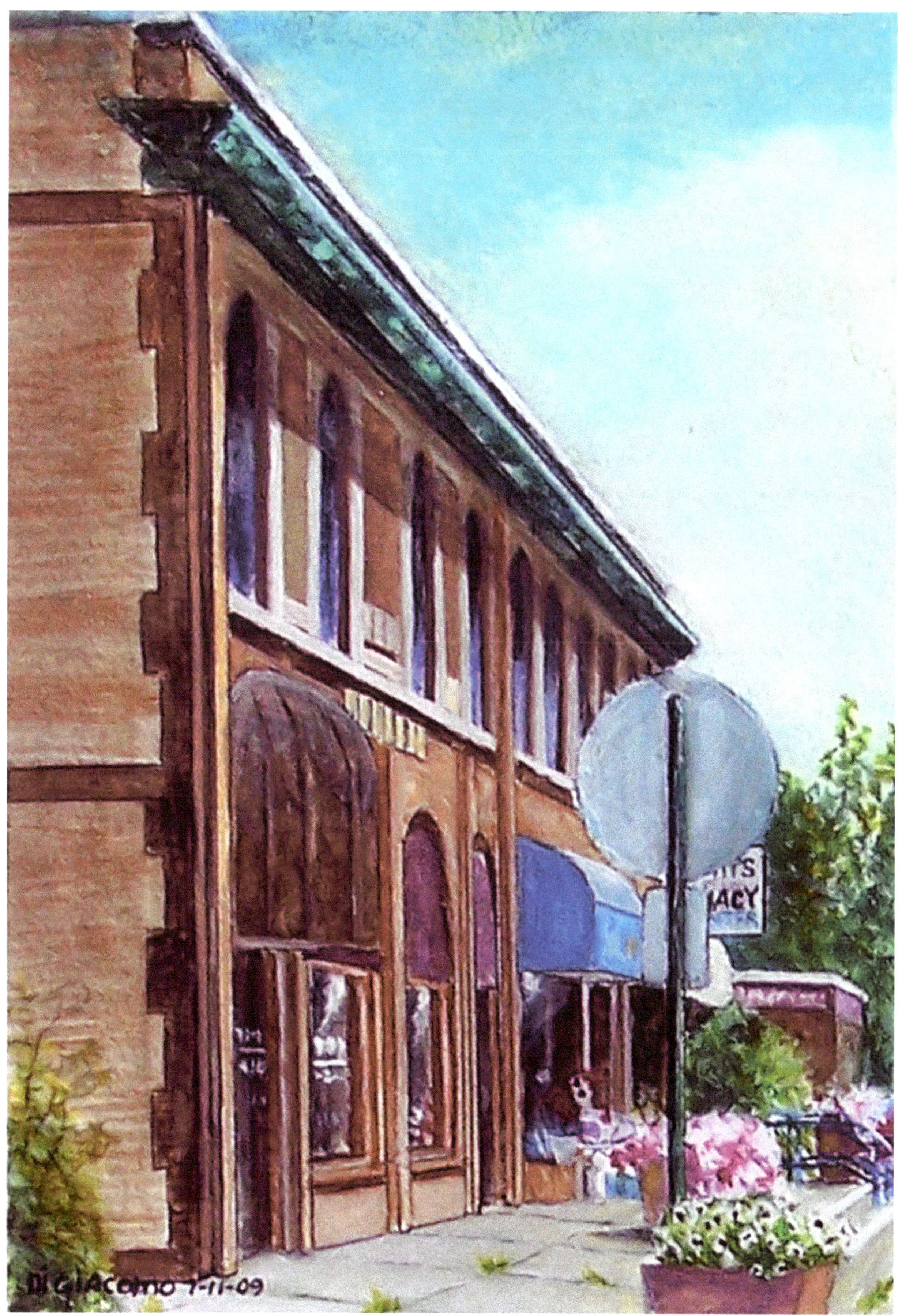

WATERCOLOR

Trees!

In my younger days I had trouble painting this subject. My trees looked like green ice cream cones with different shades of green and yellow dots. Then I realized tree shapes have a pattern which is important in identifying the species. If this is not important, a generic tree can be used but it, too, must have a pattern.

In all objects there must be three tones: a mid (or base) color, dark tones and highlights.

Sometimes superficial lighting is shown but this should be limited. I do use a camera for reference. I like to take pictures in the spring and late fall. The reason being, you can see the various stages of the tree. If you know details of the trees then it's easier to render great esthetics. (See illustration on page 15.)

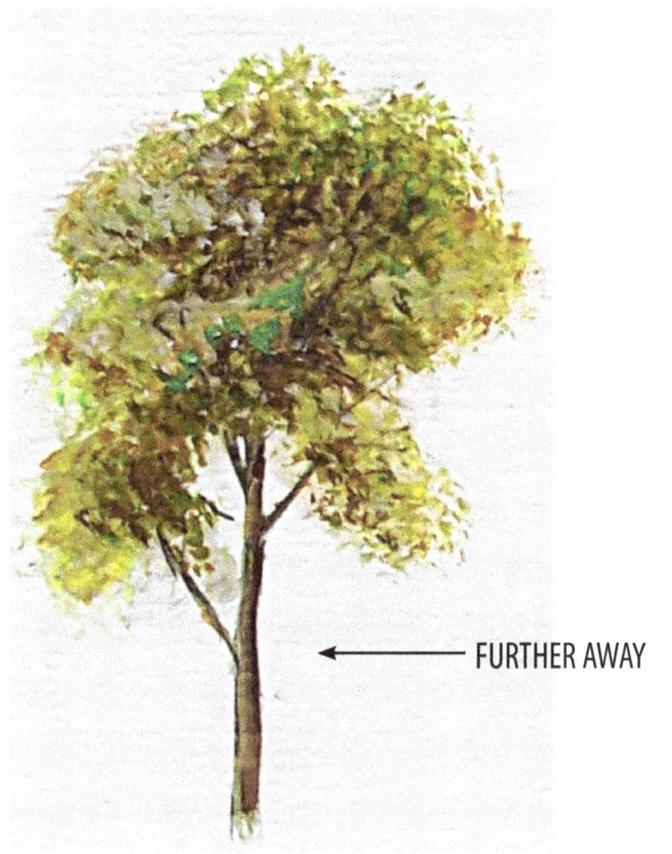

FURTHER AWAY

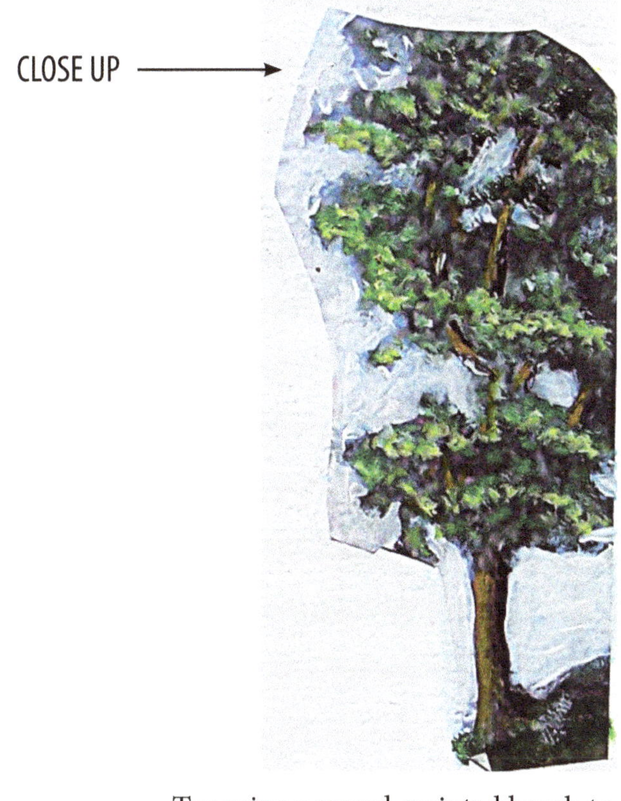

CLOSE UP

Try using a round, pointed brush to paint a leaf. Start with the point and press down while pulling back. This is used in Japanese art.

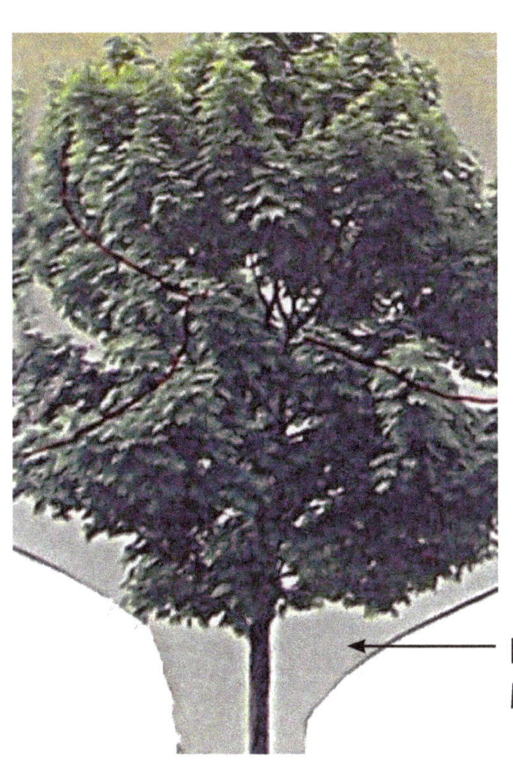

PHOTOGRAPH SHOWS FULL BLOOM, MID-SUMMER — BORING!

Another method for close up is to paint the dark hidden from sunlight first. Then the mid tones and lastly highlight the leaves.

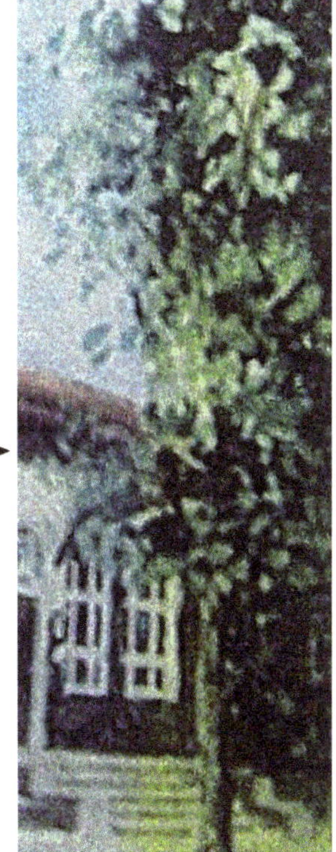

Composition, Layout and Outline

Draftsmanship is very important, so I suggest you draw objects of all shapes and sizes. (See my sample on page 17.)

If your canvass is 8-1/2" x 11"or less, and you're lazy like me, then you can use your computer and camera. Using a print and gray or black graphite paper, trace the image from the print onto the canvass. Then trace image with a **water-based** marker (do not use a permanent marker).

Look at my watercolor painting titled "MY STUDIO" on page 17. Notice the composition. You experienced artists don't need a lesson on this subject but let's review briefly anyway.

This still life follows the same rules as that of a gardener: tall objects in the back and smaller in the front. Notice the oranges are displayed in a natural manner.

To add interest, a window was put in to reveal a peek outside.

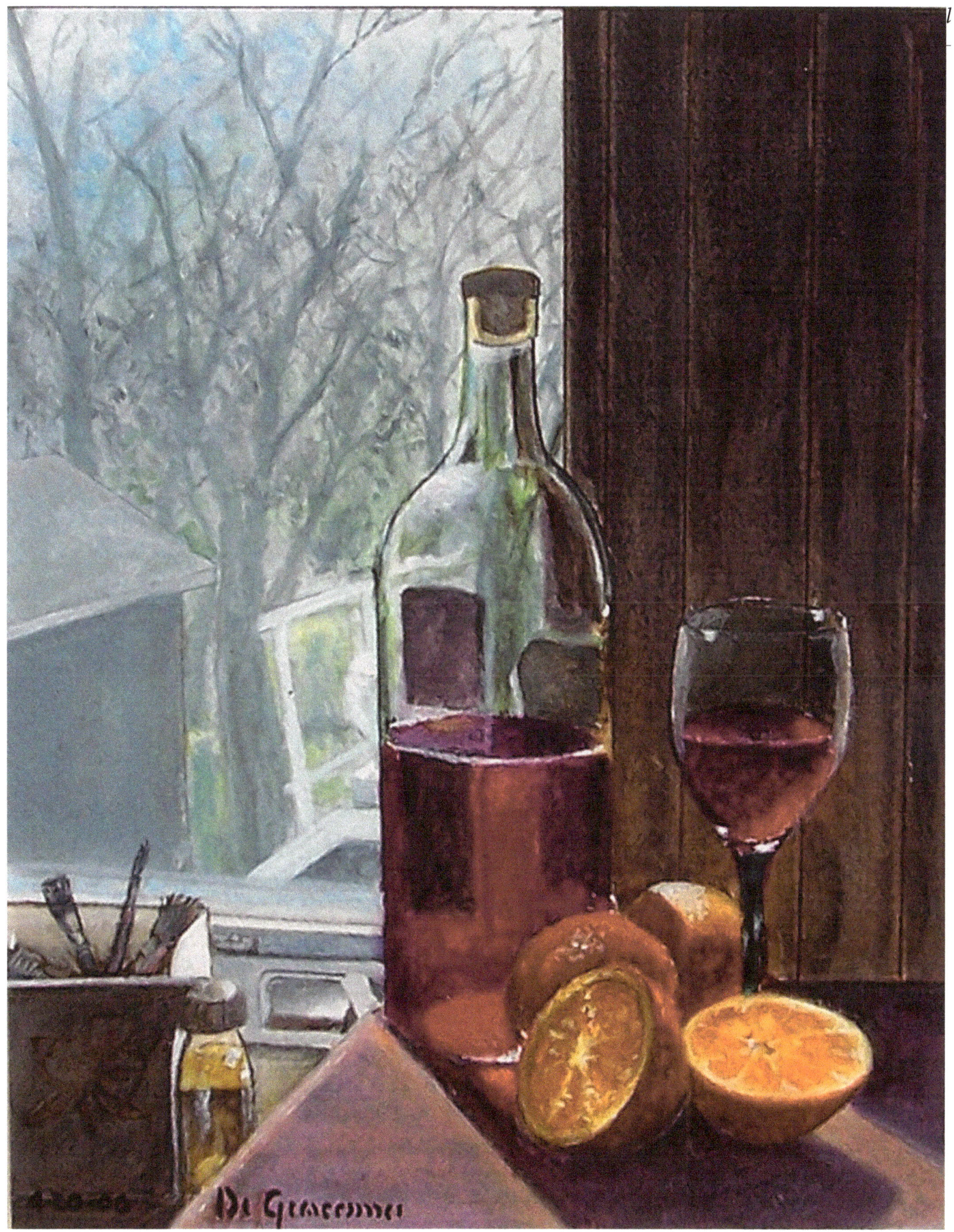

MY STUDIO

There's a method that most instructors agree on and that is to paint background and subjects together or at one time. That's okay when you're working with oils because of the slower drying time that gives you more time with your pallet. The advantage is that your painting becomes unified and balanced.

Lately I have been working with acrylics and like to use a method commercial artist and animation artists use. I paint the background completely and add the outline of the subjects in the foreground, as shown on page 19. The advantage to this method is that you can focus on detail. The disadvantage is you must know your painting will have complete balance **beforehand.**

HANDY TIP

PREPARING FOR WATERCOLOR PAINTING

I have discussed acrylic and oil painting. So now, let's prepare for Watercolor. Most instructors say to tape the 140# paper to a board, while others say to tack it. Well, I never had much luck with ether.

I tried using a 3M spray mount like you'd use for mounting photos. If you add too much spray, the painting might tear, ruining my hard work. So, I decided to use foamboard, since Styrofoam is cheap. (Hobby Lobby has sheets of 1/4-inch thick 20 x 30 foamboard for $2.49 each.) I mount my paper to the board with super 3M spray for a permanent mount, and it frames much better. This method prevents your paper from bucklling.

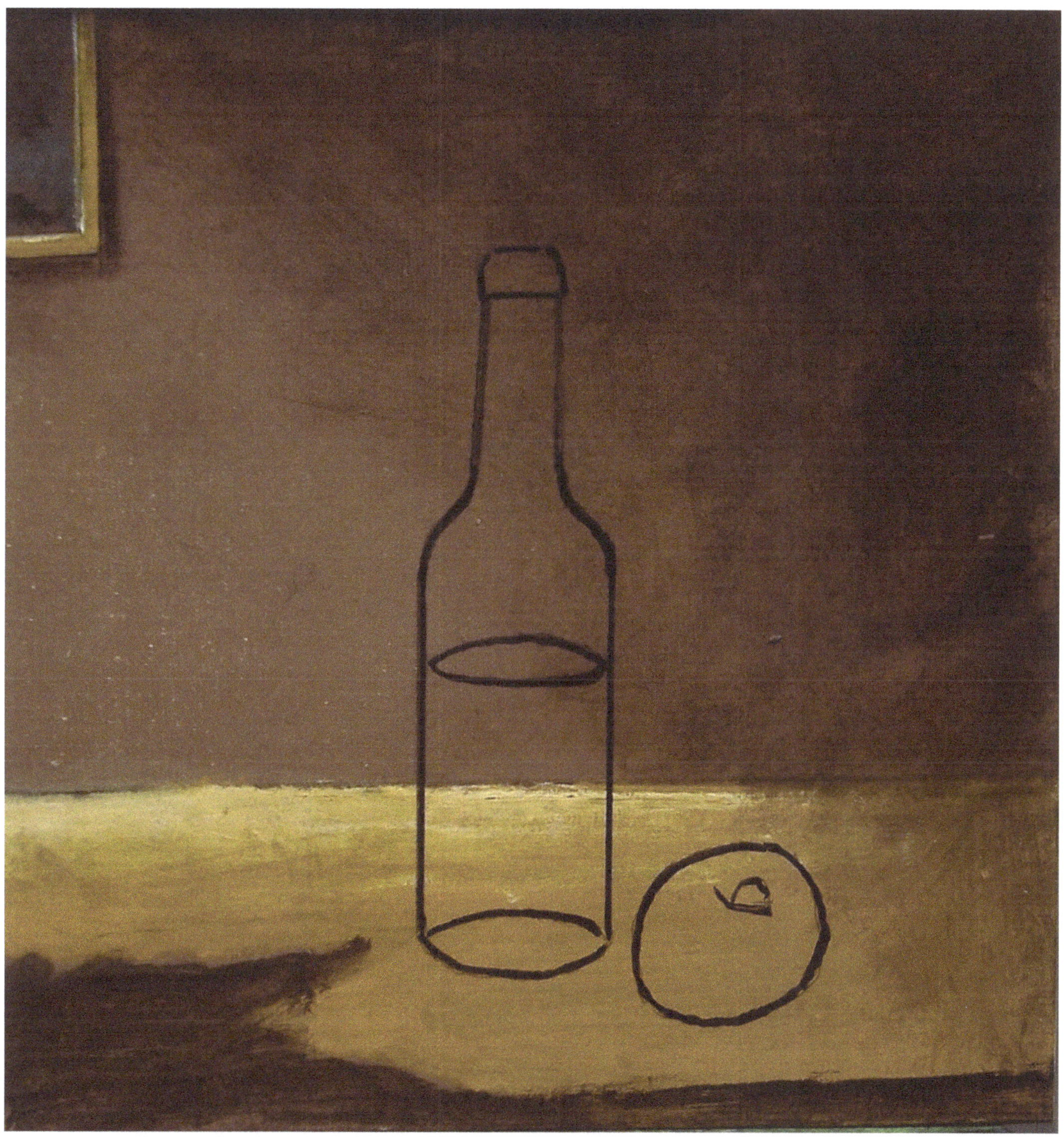

This image shows the copleted background and the outlines of the subjects in the foreground. For this image, I used Master Touch Raw Umber and Payne's Grey for the backdrop and Yellow Ochre for the base.

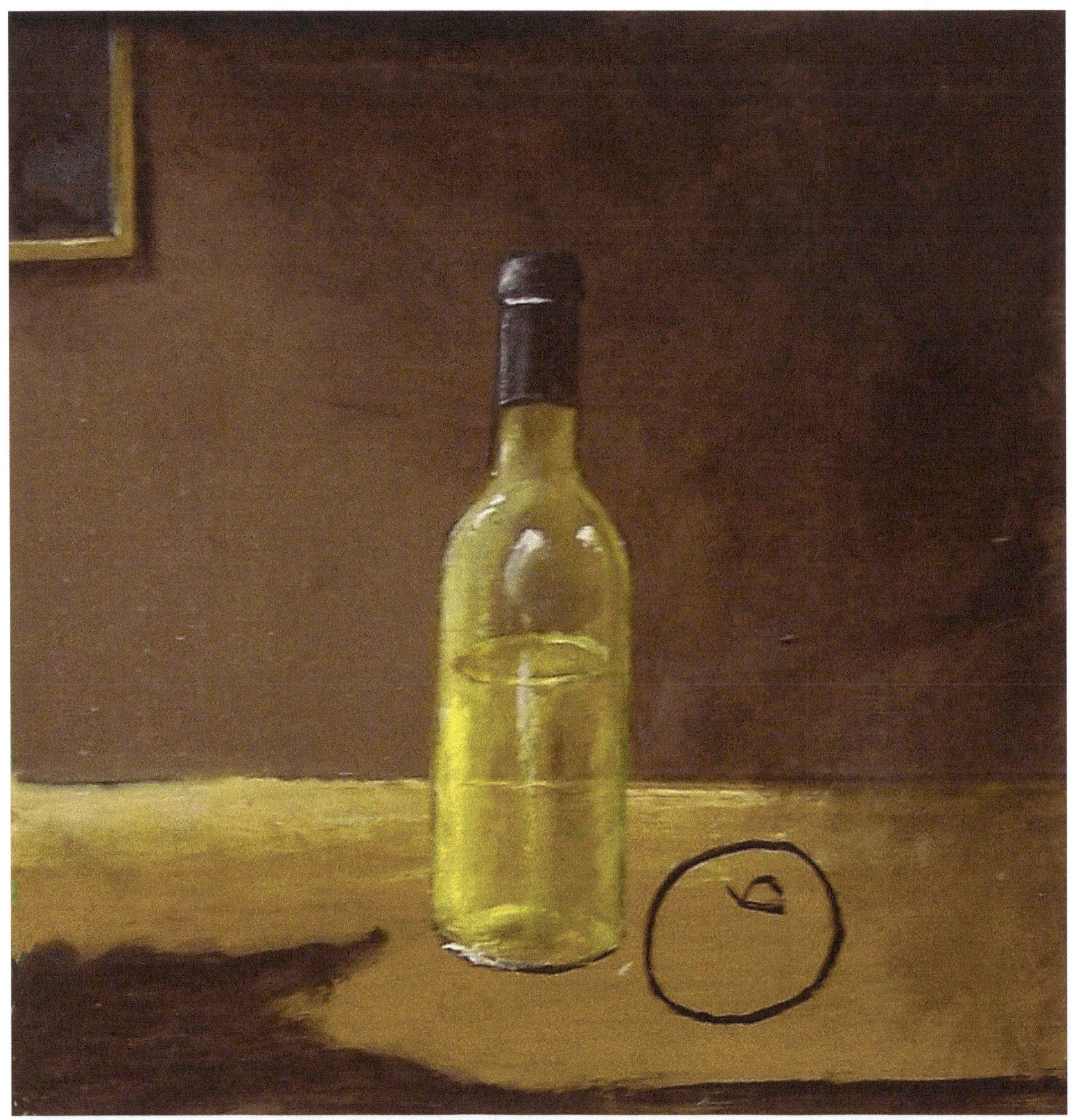

This image shows one subject completed. (I love painting glass.) It was hard for me to not overdo this bottle. Notice the outline of the second object. Here, I used Cadmium Yellow, Neutral Grey and white. Tint the bottle with yellow grey mix and rub it in, followed with a lighter yellow for the liquid.

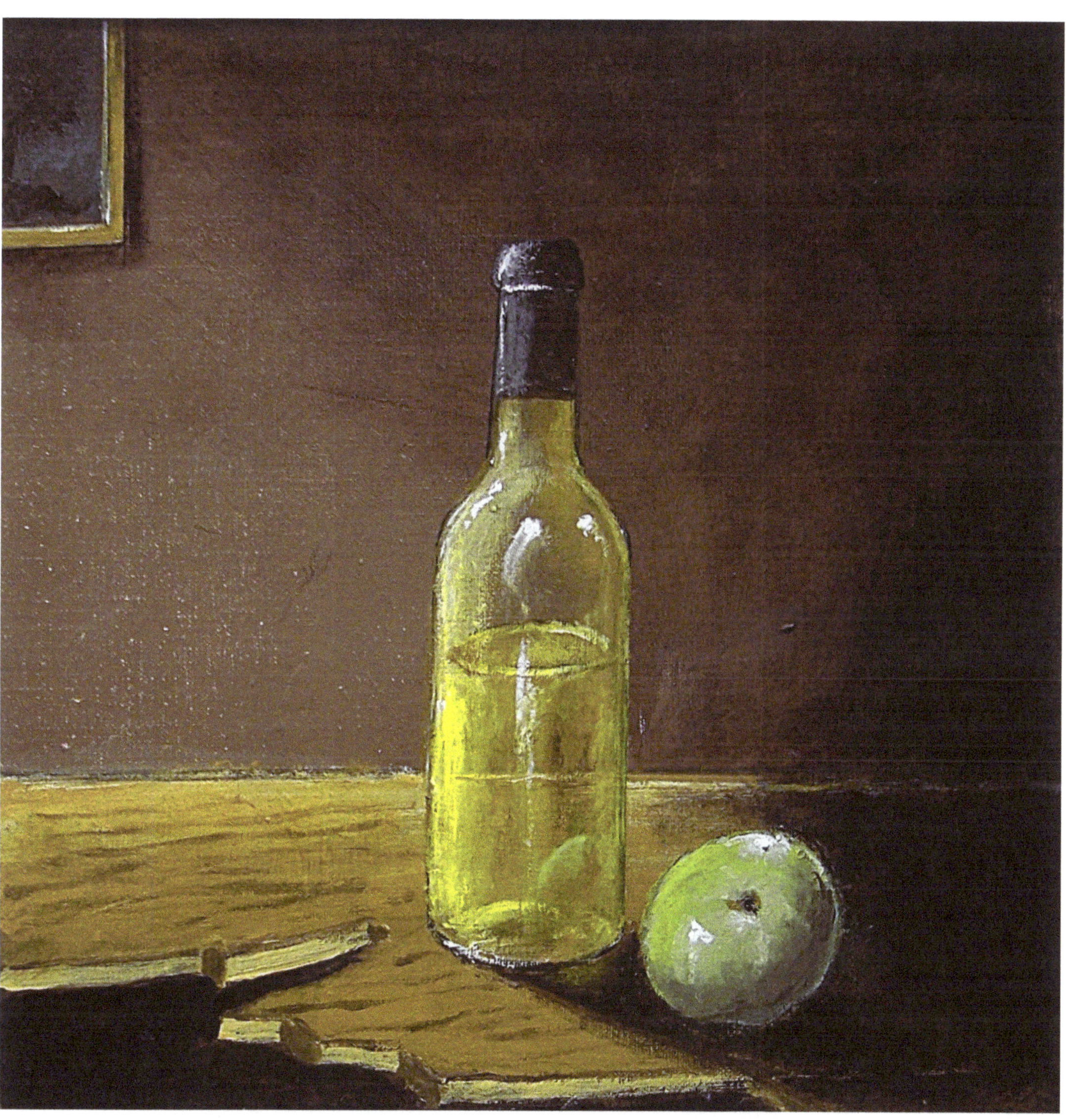

The finished painting. Notice the changes and tweaking done a little here and there. But I did make a mistake, which you will benefit from. When painting a light subject you should have a dark background. Better yet, like the old masters, have your subject come out from the dark. To balance and correct my mistake, I added a dark base.

Here I used Payne's Grey for the lower left . For the apple, I used Cadmium Yellow, Grass Green, white and raw umber.

Now a word of encouragement. If you think you are doing badly, stop! If you could see how I began, you would not believe I did these illustrations.

Many art instructors recommend painting quickly. That's fine, if you know where you're going! I say take your time and play with different colors, etc. This is how you learn.

Review some of the things we just discussed about shadows by examining the tip below.

HANDY TIP

SHADOWS WITH INDIRECT LIGHTING

Previously we learned the colors required to paint a shadow, but now let's see what happens in indirect lighting outside.

The illustration on the right shows a shadow in direct lighting. The subject on the left shows what indirect lighting would look like. Indirect lighting may occur when light rays are split due to atmospheric changes like a fast moving cloud or light coming through trees.It can be interesting, but in this case it does not add to the painting.

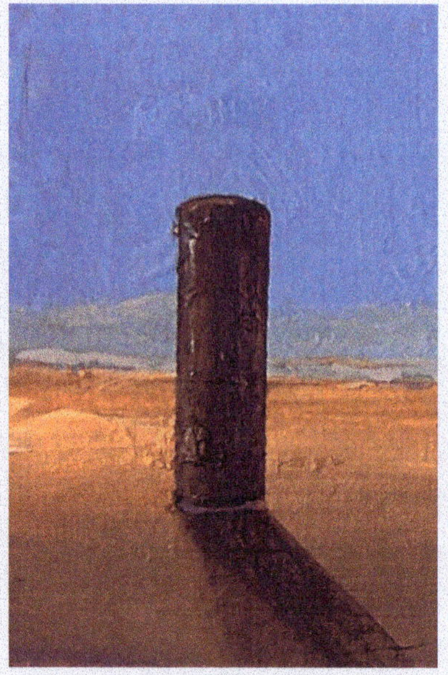

INDIRECT LIGHT

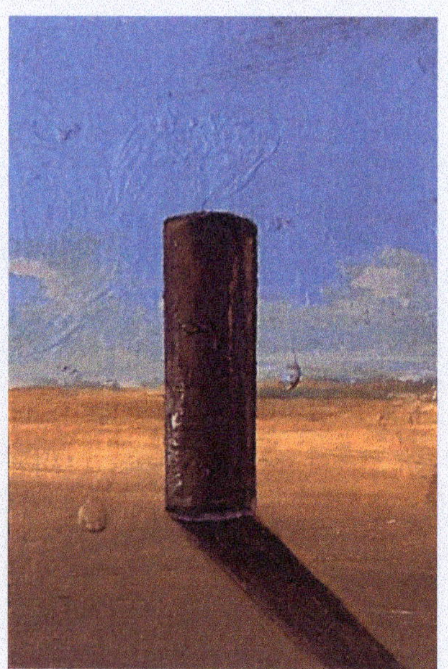

DIRECT LIGHT

Painting Glass

When painting glass, be sure not to overdo it. I know you want to add more highlights, etc. but it will defeat your purpose. Just outline the object and let the background through. Strategically add the highlights with a dry brush, which is needed here.

In commercial art, I would use cardboard and cut out the subject then trace it onto the canvas (no wax pencil or permanent marker). Then retrace with a fine brush and light gray or light blue paint. (See the illustrations on pages 23-27.)

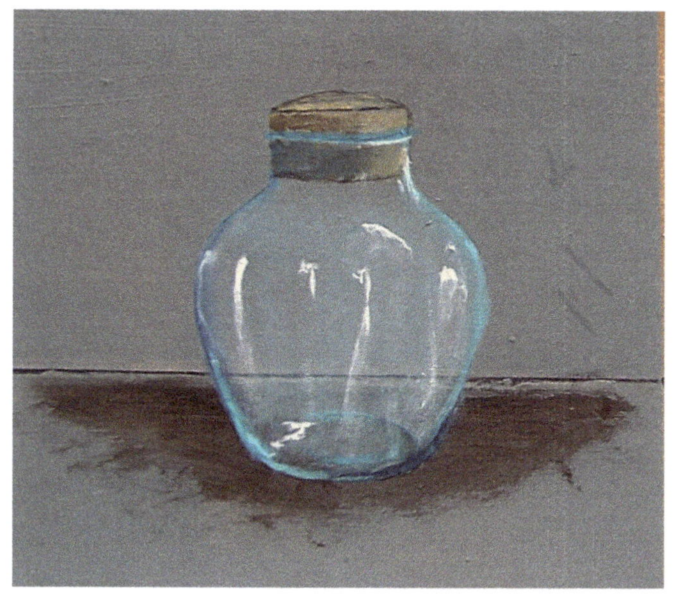

This view was actually copied from a photo. Notice the highlights are superficial and do not add anything to the beauty of this delicate vase. The lighting was poorly placed.

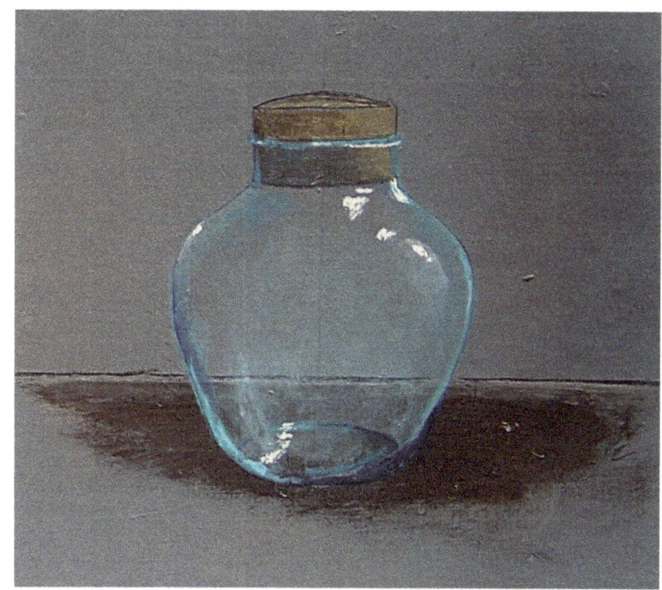

This view proves less is more. That is, a few highlights strategically located are all that is required. To tint the glass, I used the outline colors with a touch of light grey, and rubbed with a paper towel. THIS IS A DRY BRUSH RUB. This creates a delicate glass vase.

For both vases here I used acrylica Cerulean Blue, Aqua Green, and Natural Grey, for the outline. Also Paynes Grey was used for the dark tones.

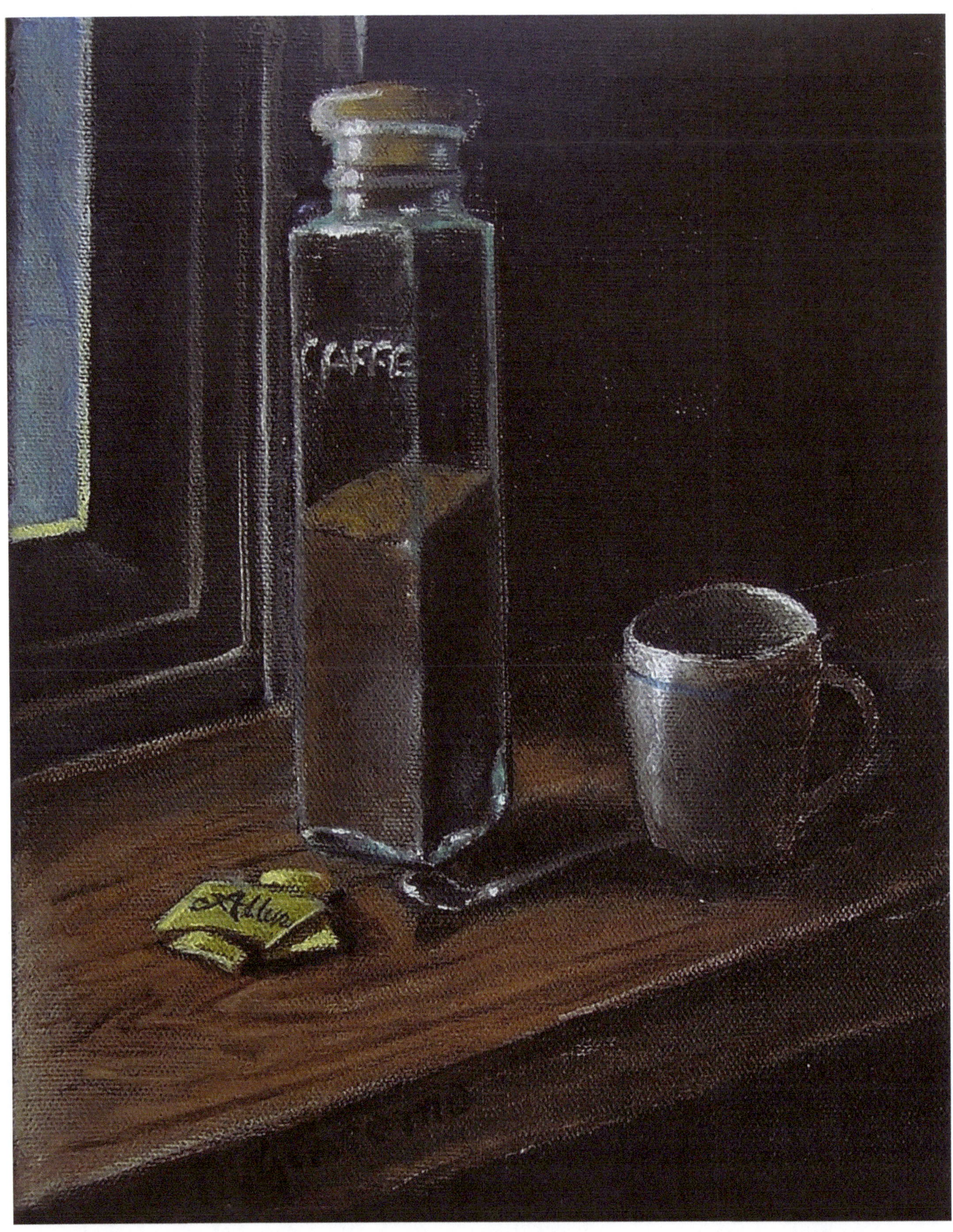
CAFFE
Adler

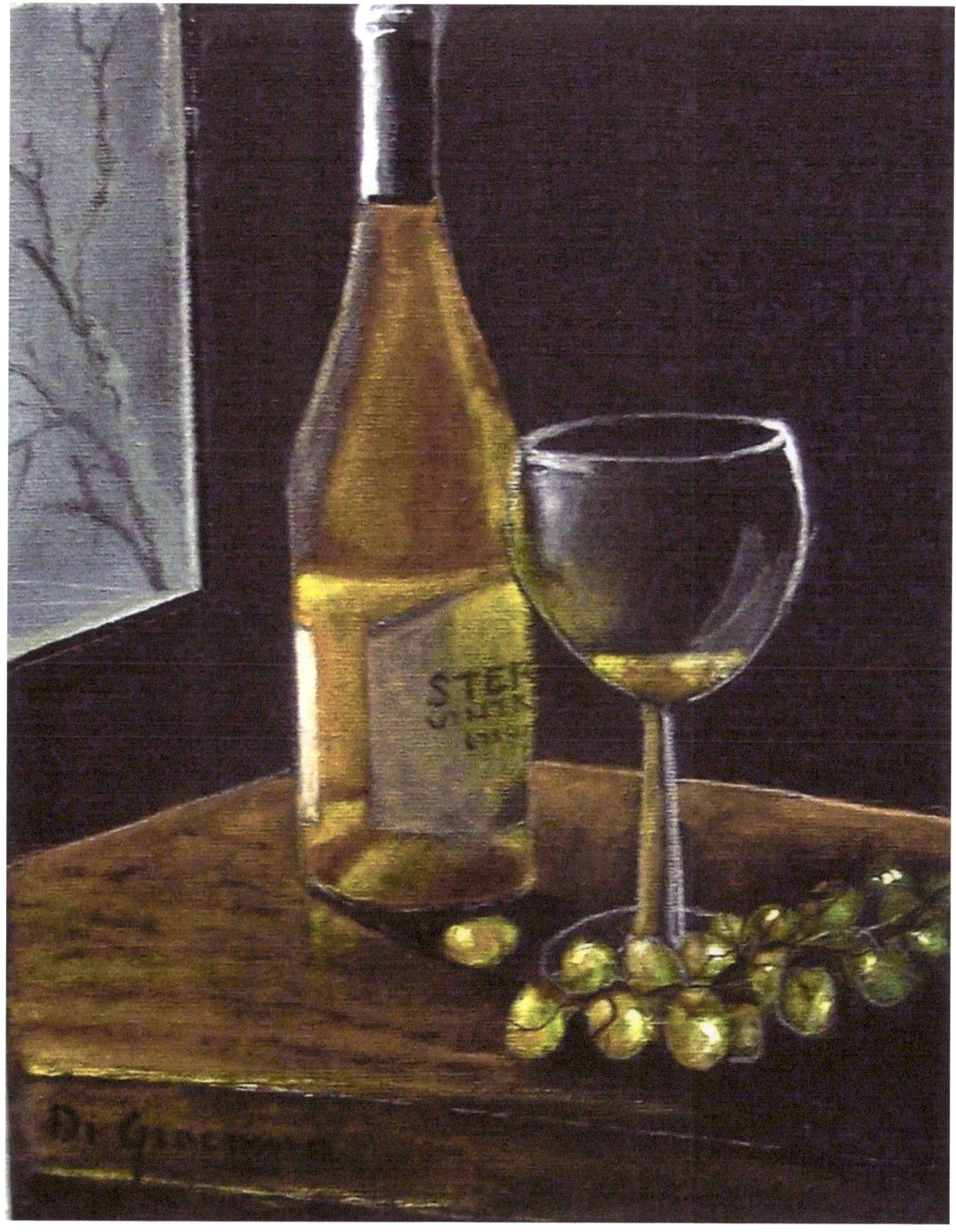

STE
Dr Gierowsch

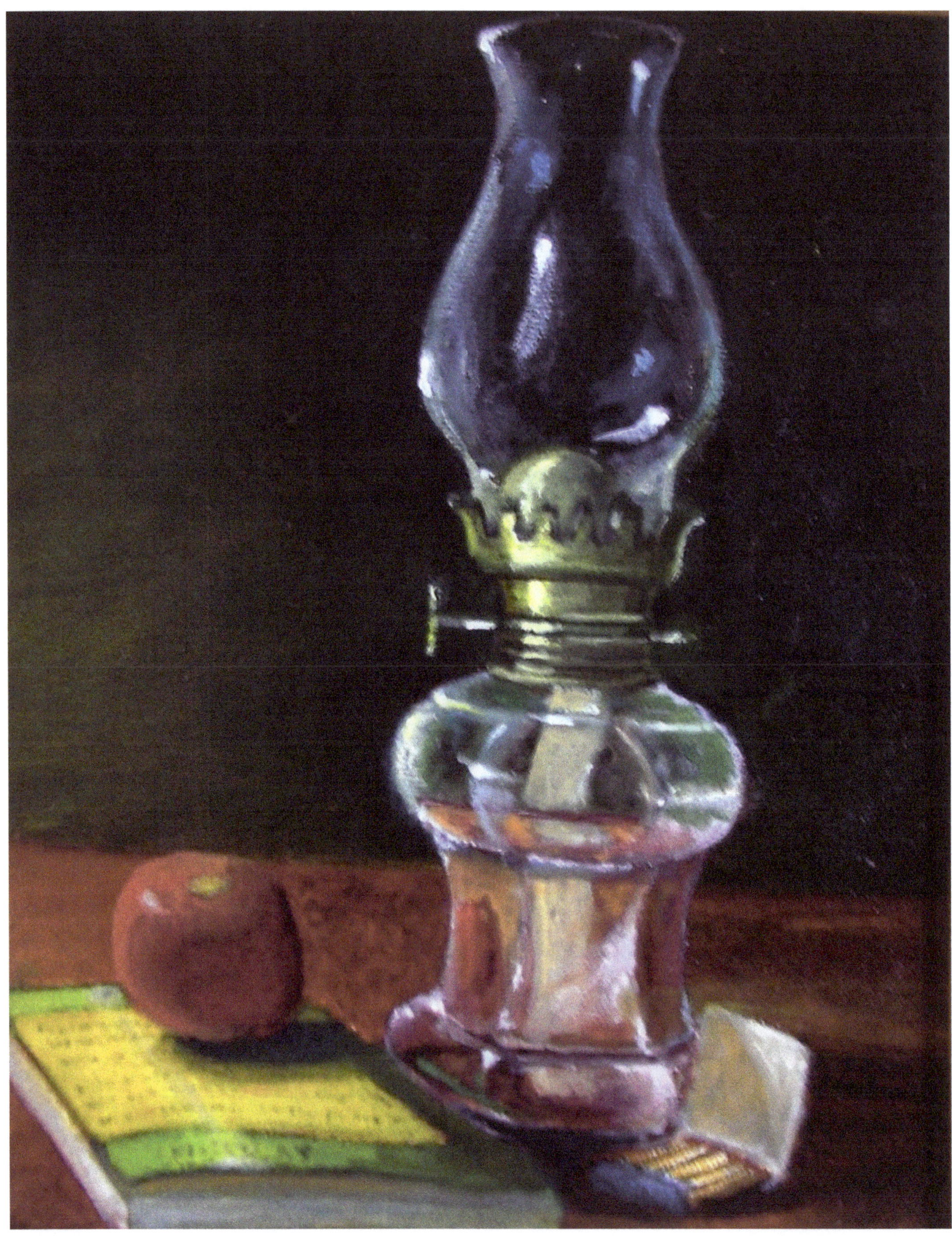

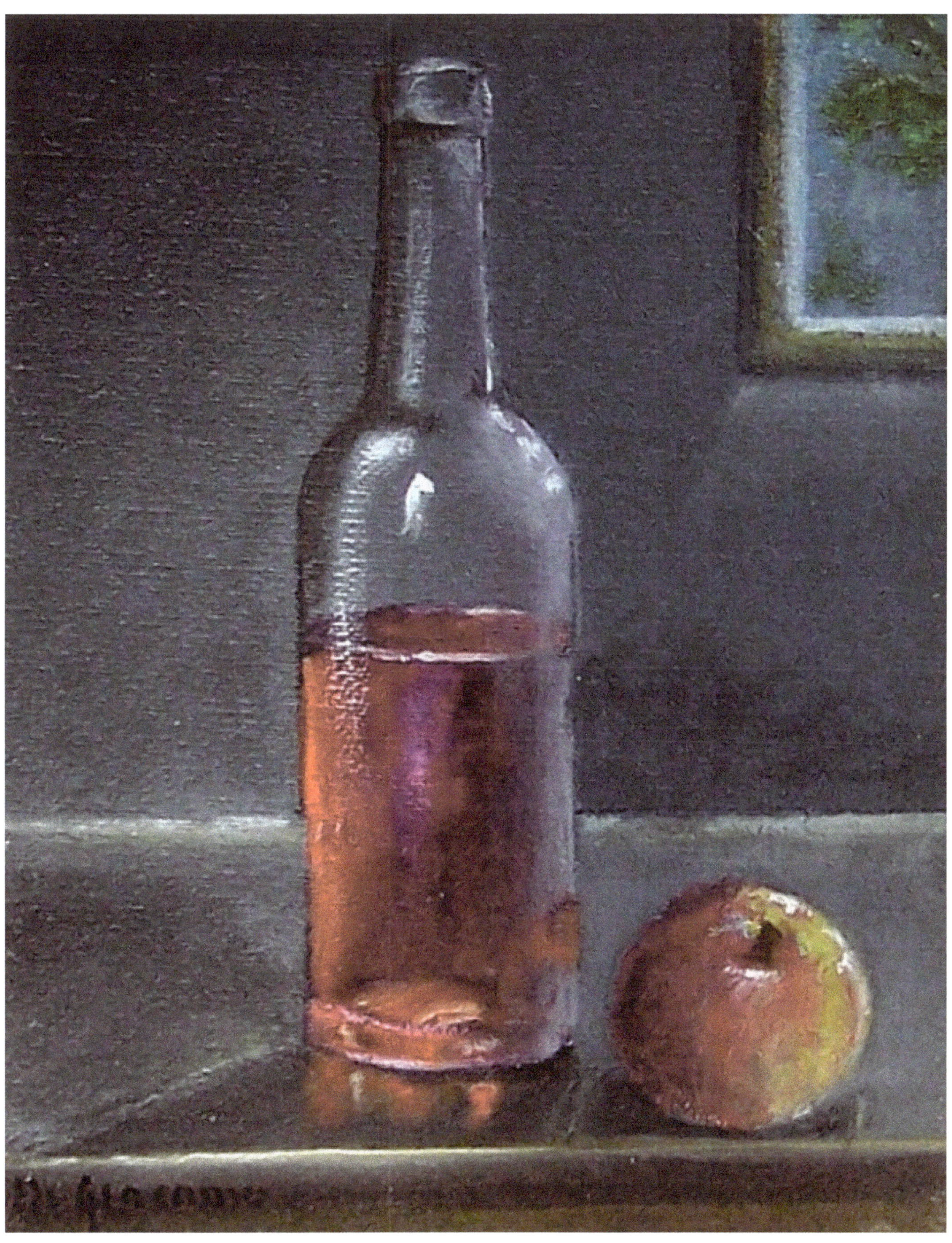

You may have noticed that I call colors by their common names instead of their chemical names. The reason for this is that an artist <u>should be able to recognize color composition first</u>, then learn the proper names. The artist should see the color combination of the blue and red in purple as an example, and so on.

Check out the illustrations on pages 29-31.

STUDY TO IMPROVE

I would like to take a moment here to add some things that might help you. I find that if you study how things are made or created by nature with a analytical mind, it will aid you tremendously as an artist. Get all the knowledge you can, and your art will reveal much of you.

Study color mixtures, and become like the color mixer at the home improvement stores. If you paint the sky, learn all the different cloud types and their shapes. For trees learn the different species. There's nothing better than seeing subjects that look real!

Moving water, like the angry sea., will be difficult to create. This is where a camera comes in handy. As mentioned before, study how trees grow and how the wheat fields bend in the wind. In other words, be aware, study the objects that surround you and your paintings will benefit.

Good luck!

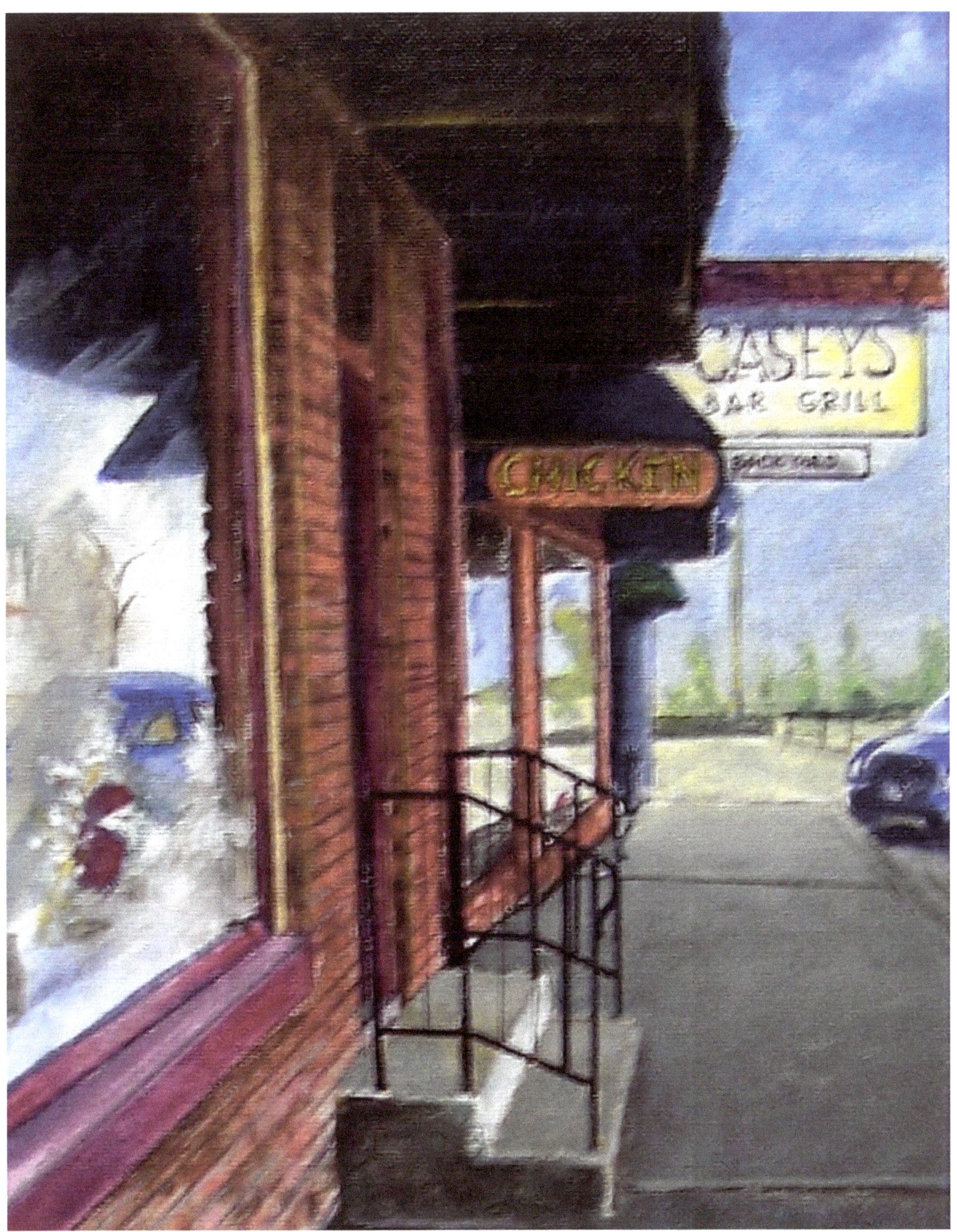

CASEYS
BAR GRILL
CHICKEN

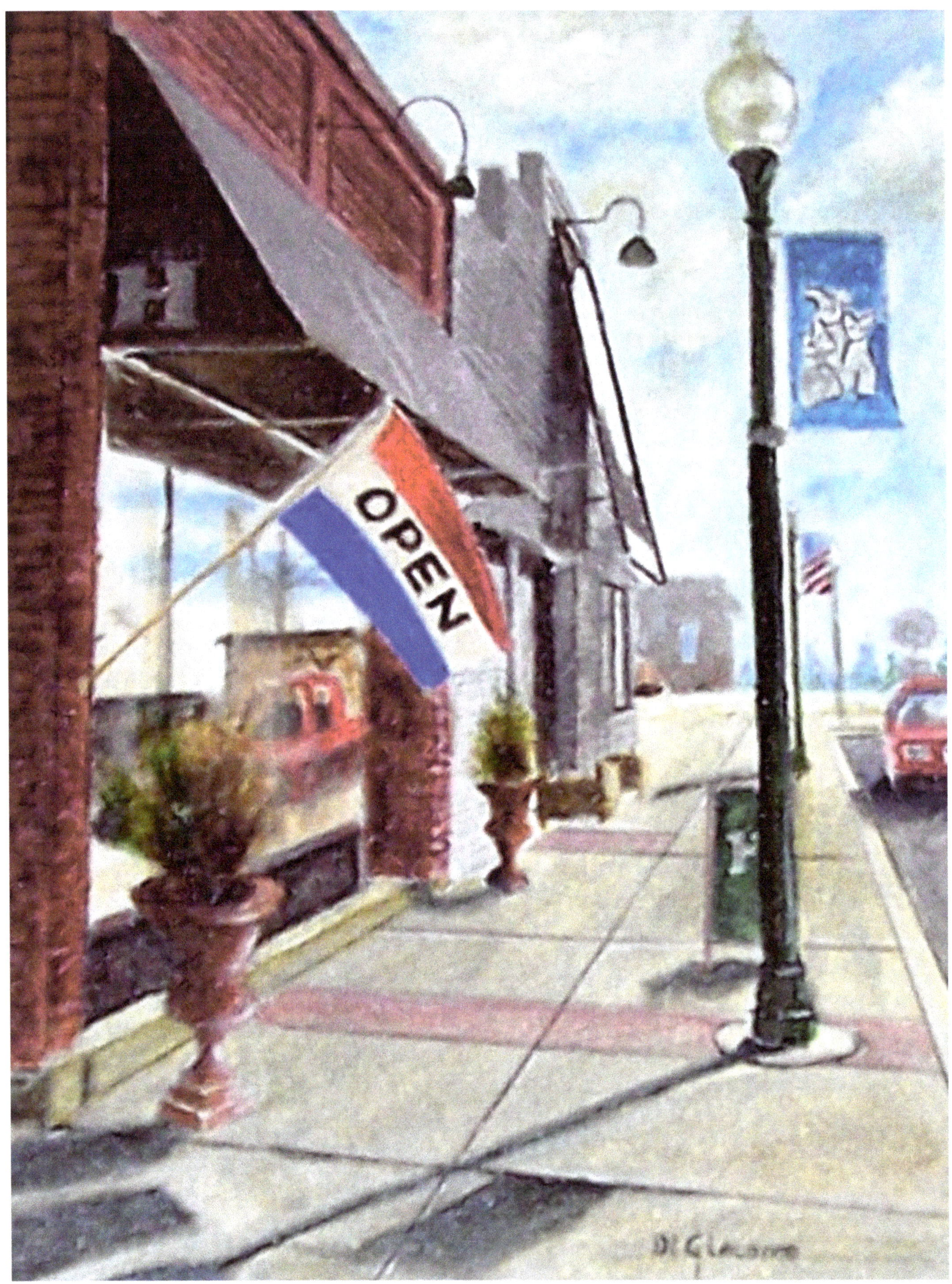

H
OPEN
DiGiacomo

Gray All Colors

BRICK WALL

LIGHT POST

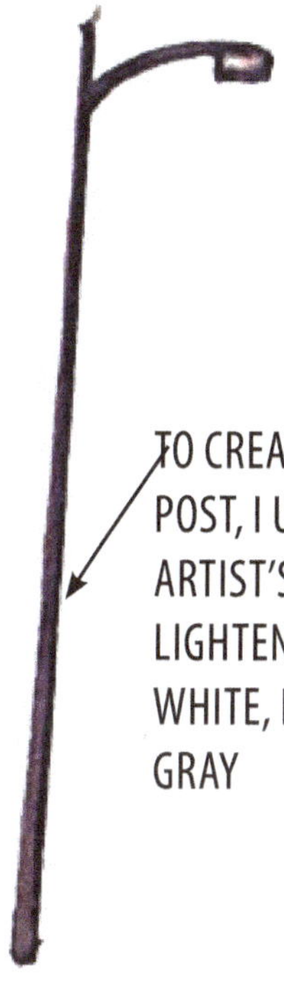

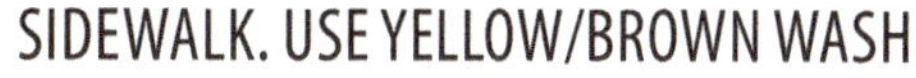

TO CREATE THE LIGHT POST, I USED AN ARTIST'S PEN, THEN LIGHTENED IT WITH WHITE, BROWN AND GRAY

MORE
GRAY
REQUIRED

SIDEWALK. USE YELLOW/BROWN WASH.

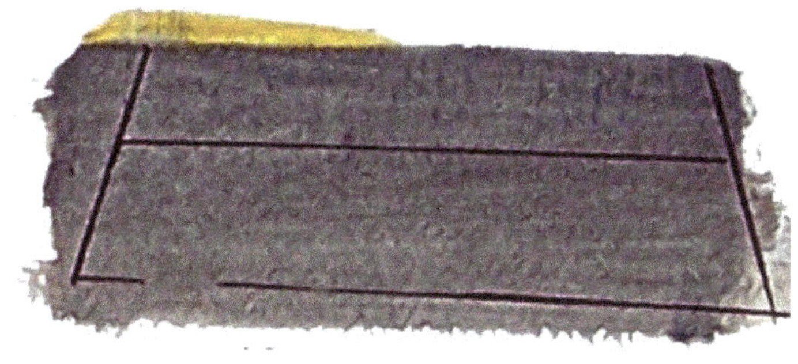

TO CREATE THE BRICKS, FIRST BLOTCH THE COLORS.
LET IT DRY. WET A BRUSH AND BRUSH ALL OVER..
COLORS USED: BROWN, YELLOW, RED

GRAY /BROWN ALL OVER

Scenery Composition

To me a most interesting scene painting is having the subject in a backdrop of three important elements: water, land and sky. Check out the painting below. The barn, trees, and shrubs are actually there.
I added a pond to the painting that doesn't really exist for interest.

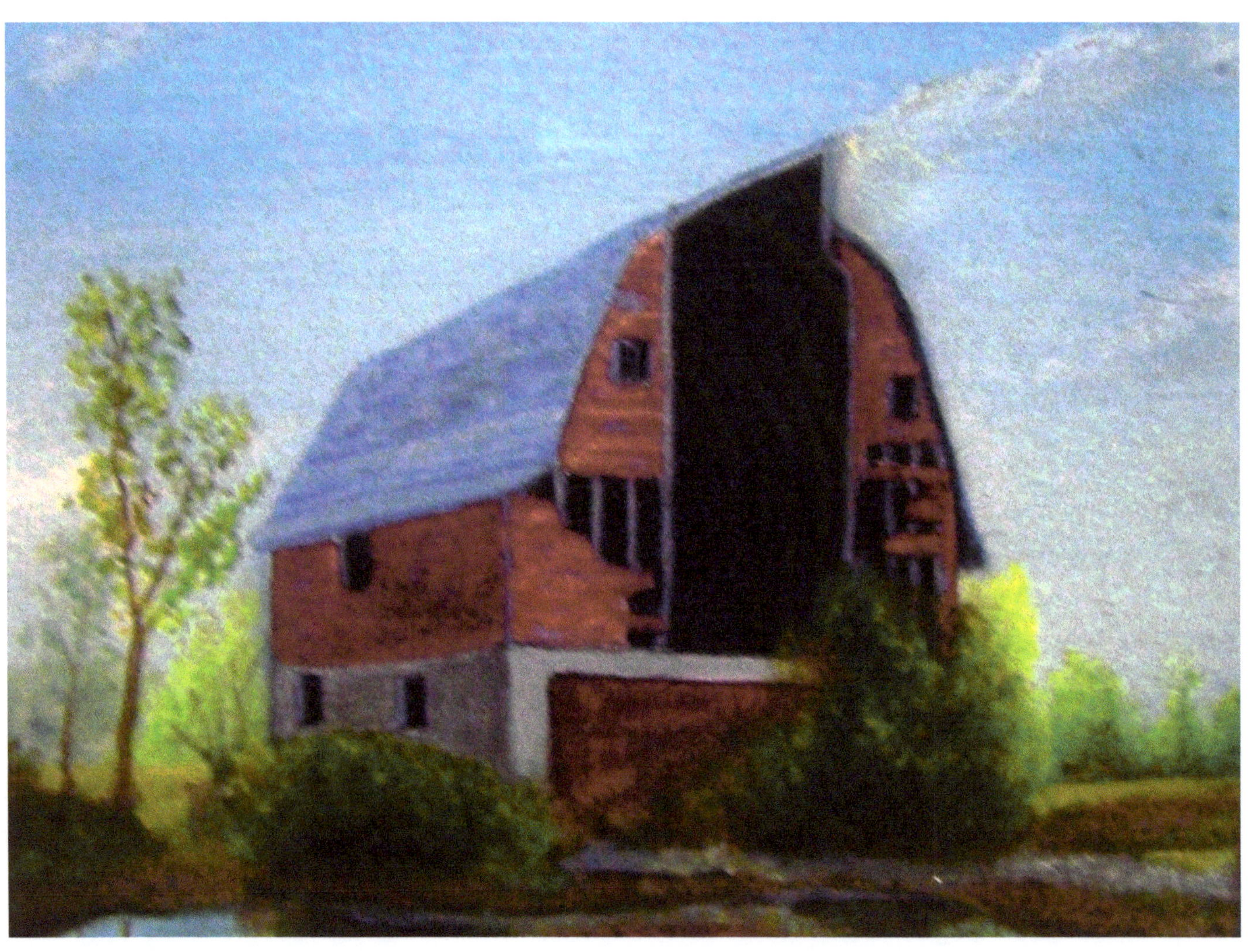

Special Effects

I wanted to do something different so I elected to spray-paint the entire canvas with flat black or dark brown. When it was dry, I laid a light gray graphite paper over the canvas and traced my subject onto the canvas.

Picture's 1 (below) has a dark brown canvas, and pictures 2 (page 34) and 3 (page 35) have a black canvas. Give it a try it was fun.

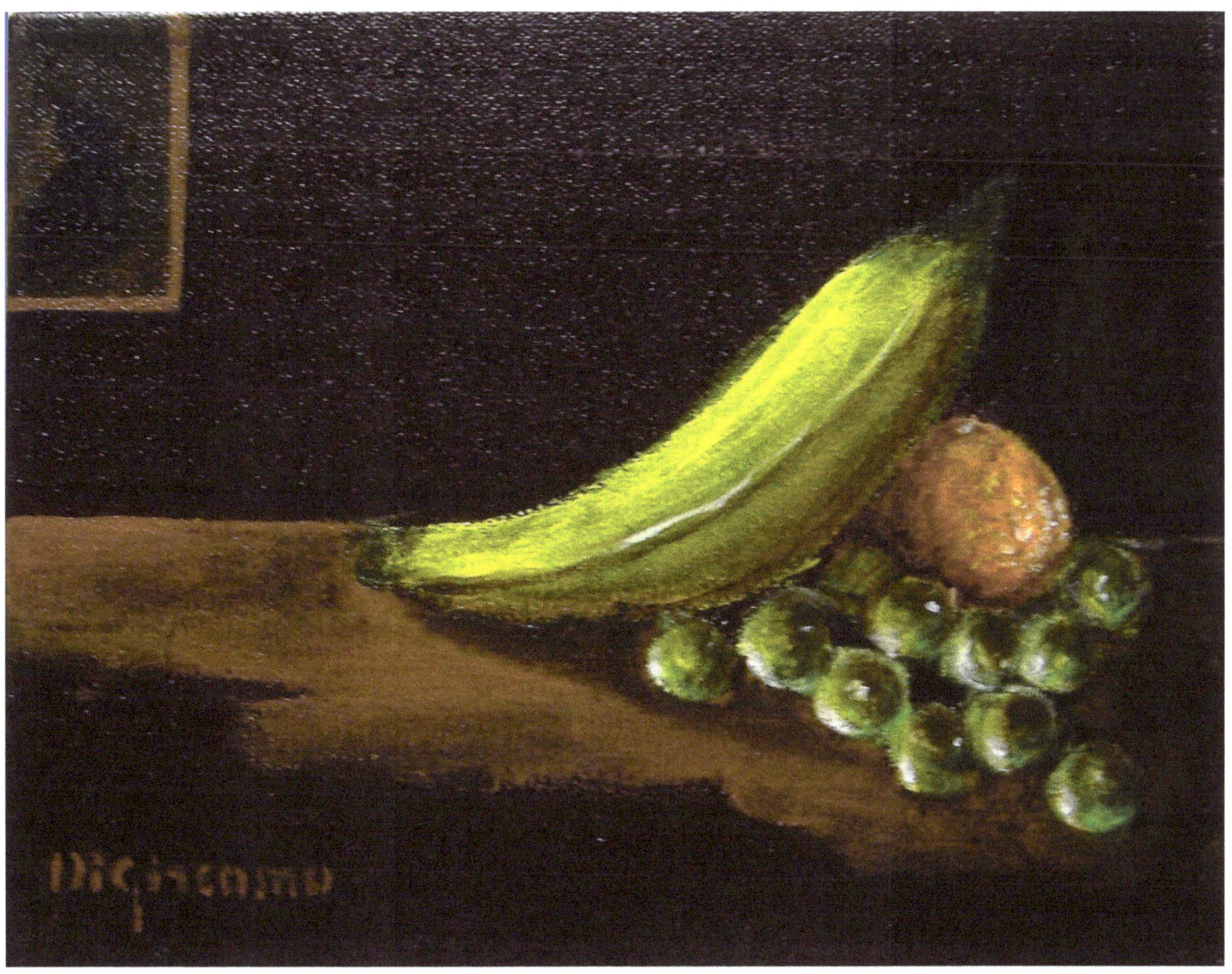

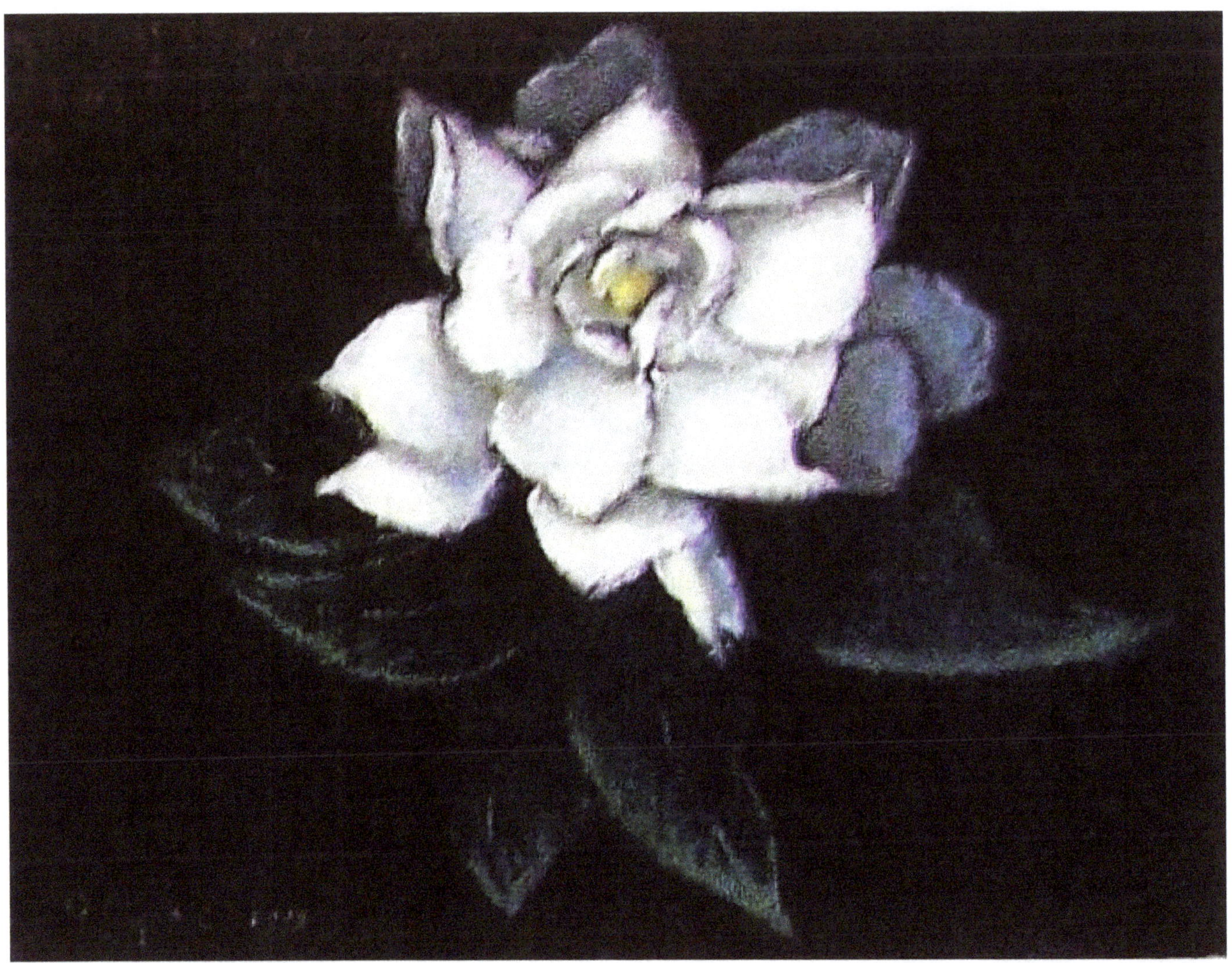

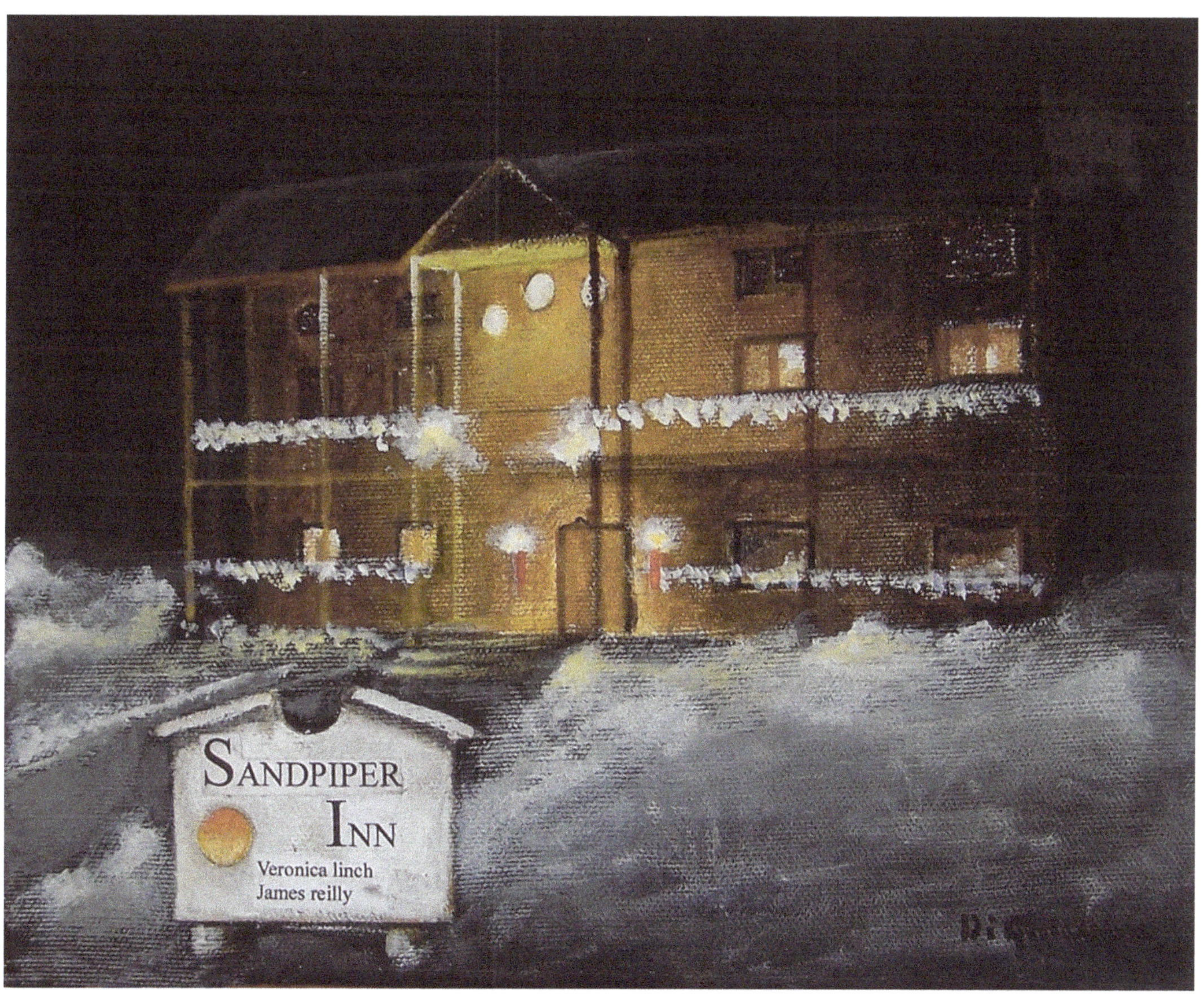
SANDPIPER
INN
Veronica linch
James reilly

No Rules

Once in a while, I like to just doodle with no rules. I just paint in a carefree way and don't worry about doing a masterpiece. It's great to do this once in a while. Sometimes, you learn techniques not known to you before. Plus, it's relaxing. The painting on page 37 was done with acrylic on a black canvas.

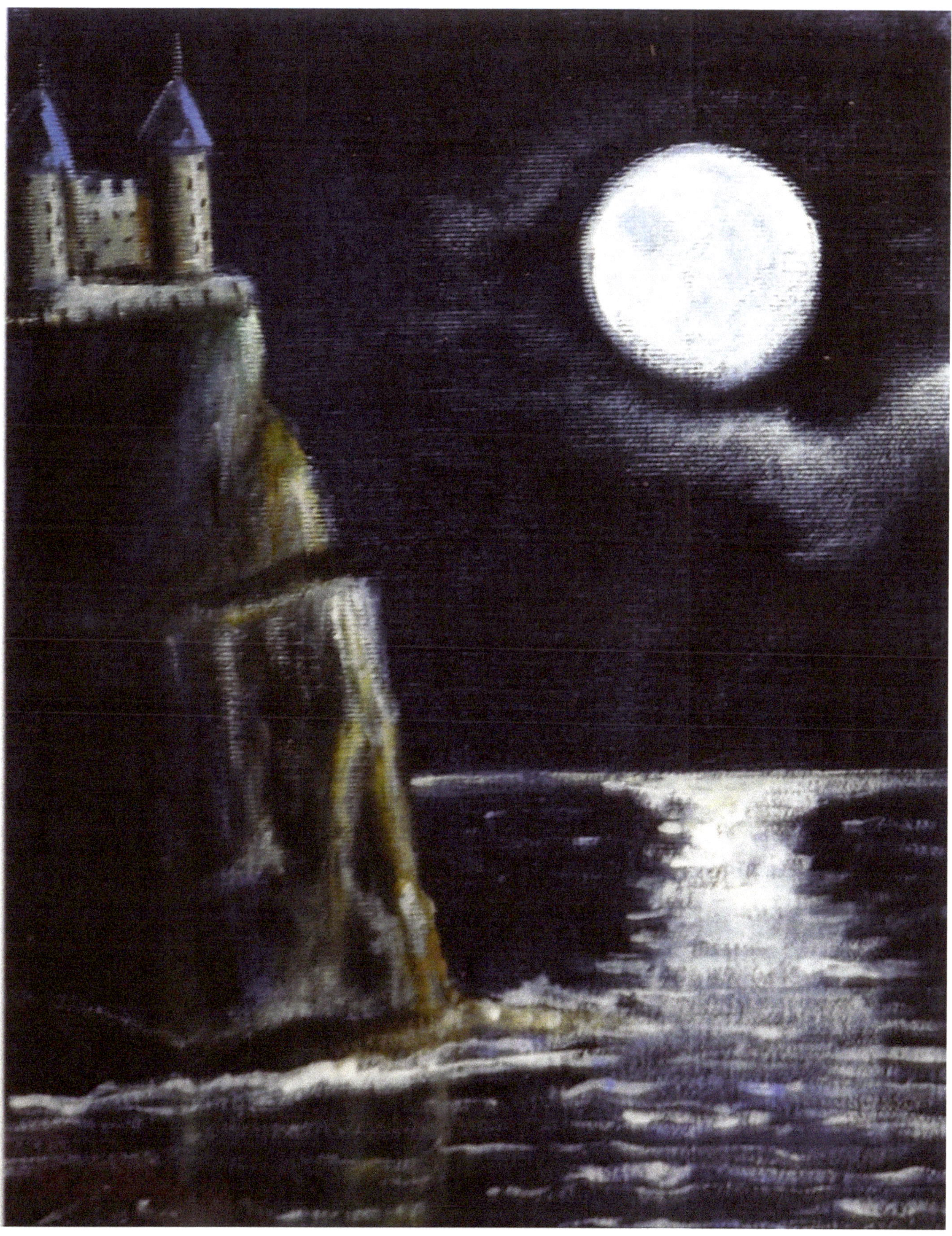

Sketches

S ketch! Sketch! Sketch! The more you do, the better your draftsmanship. This is so important because it increases your "eye-mind coordination."

The sketch below and on pages 39-45 I did while serving in the US Army in Korea in 1961.

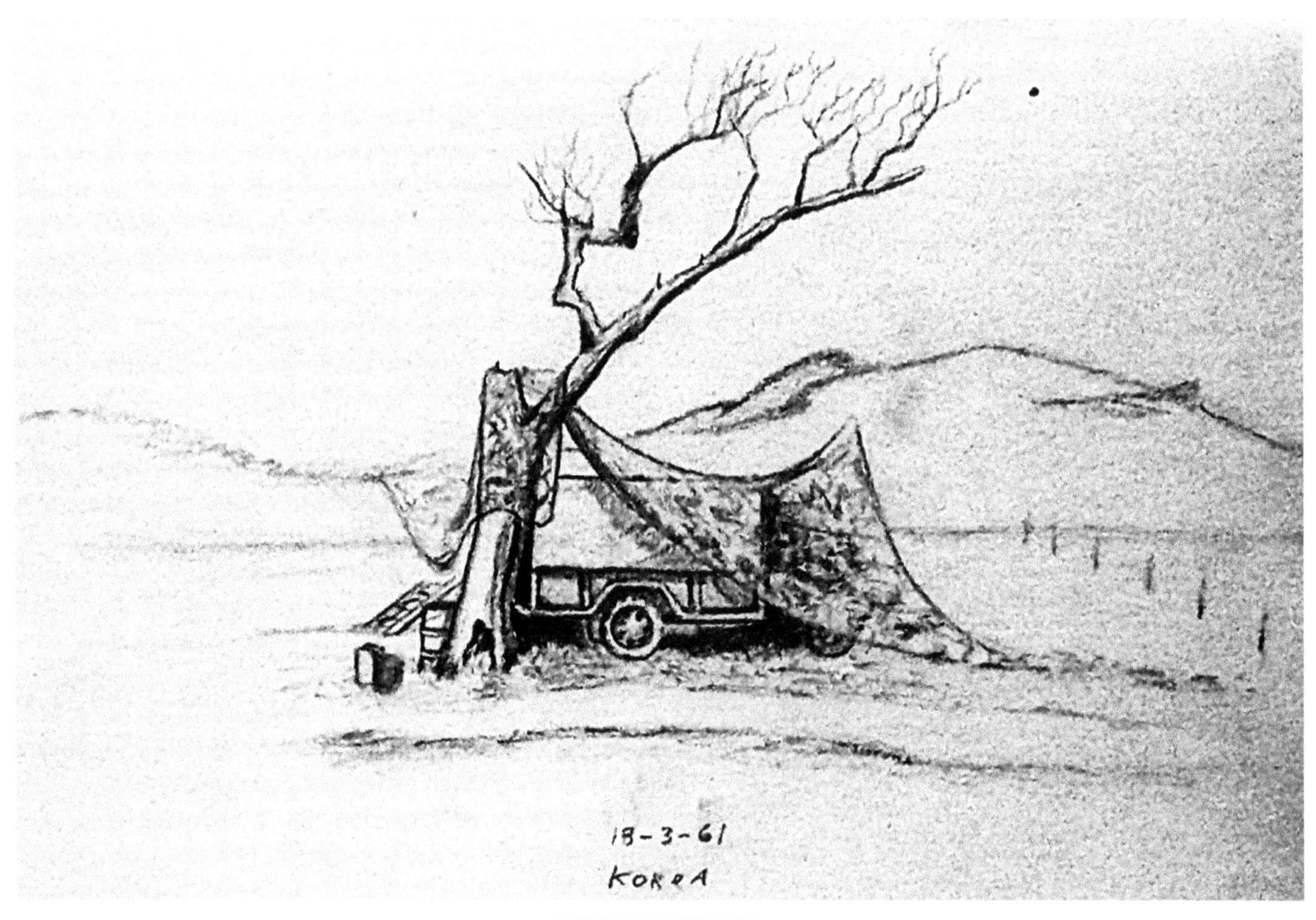

FIELD MANUEVERS

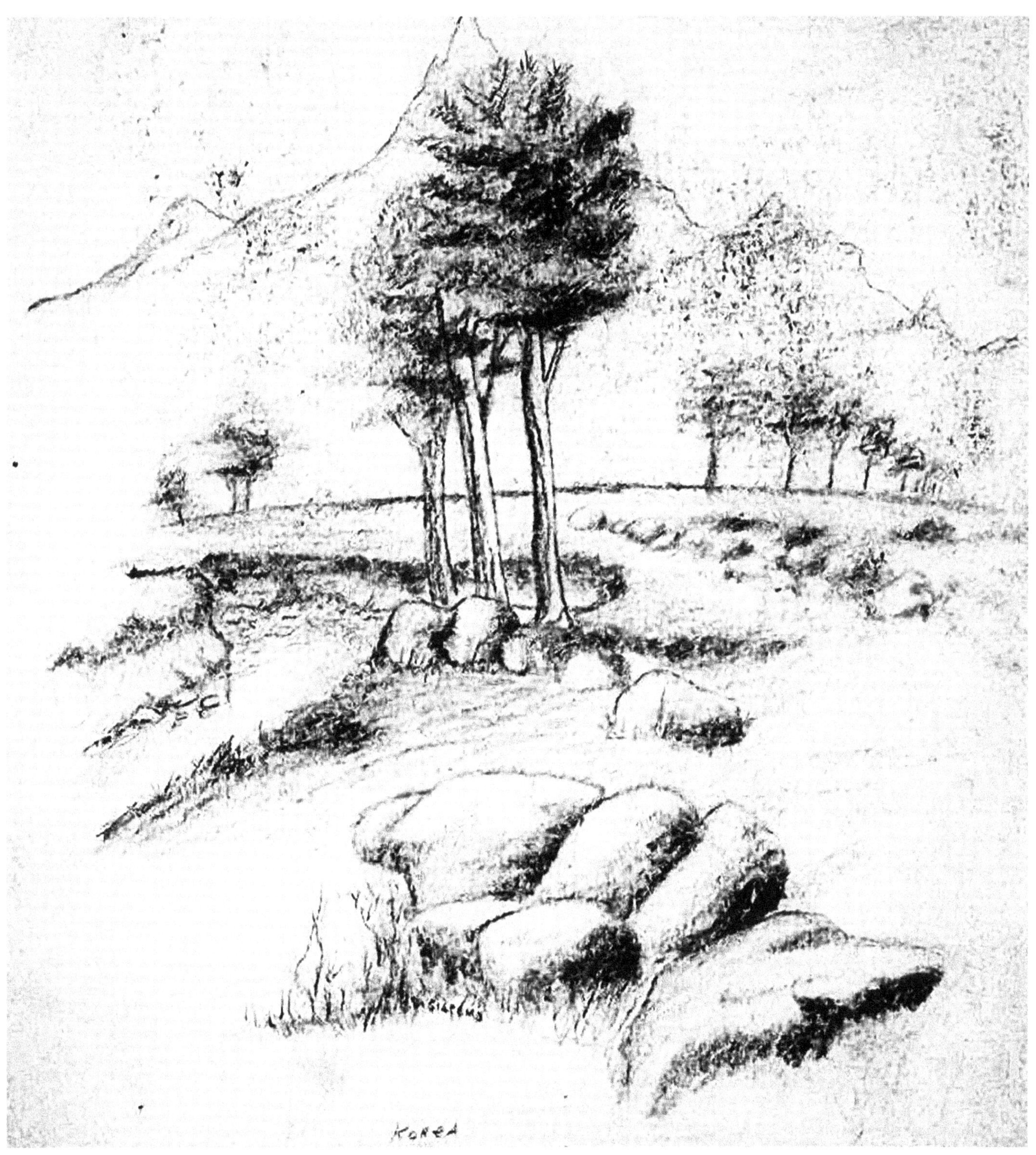

KOREAN COUNTRYSIDE

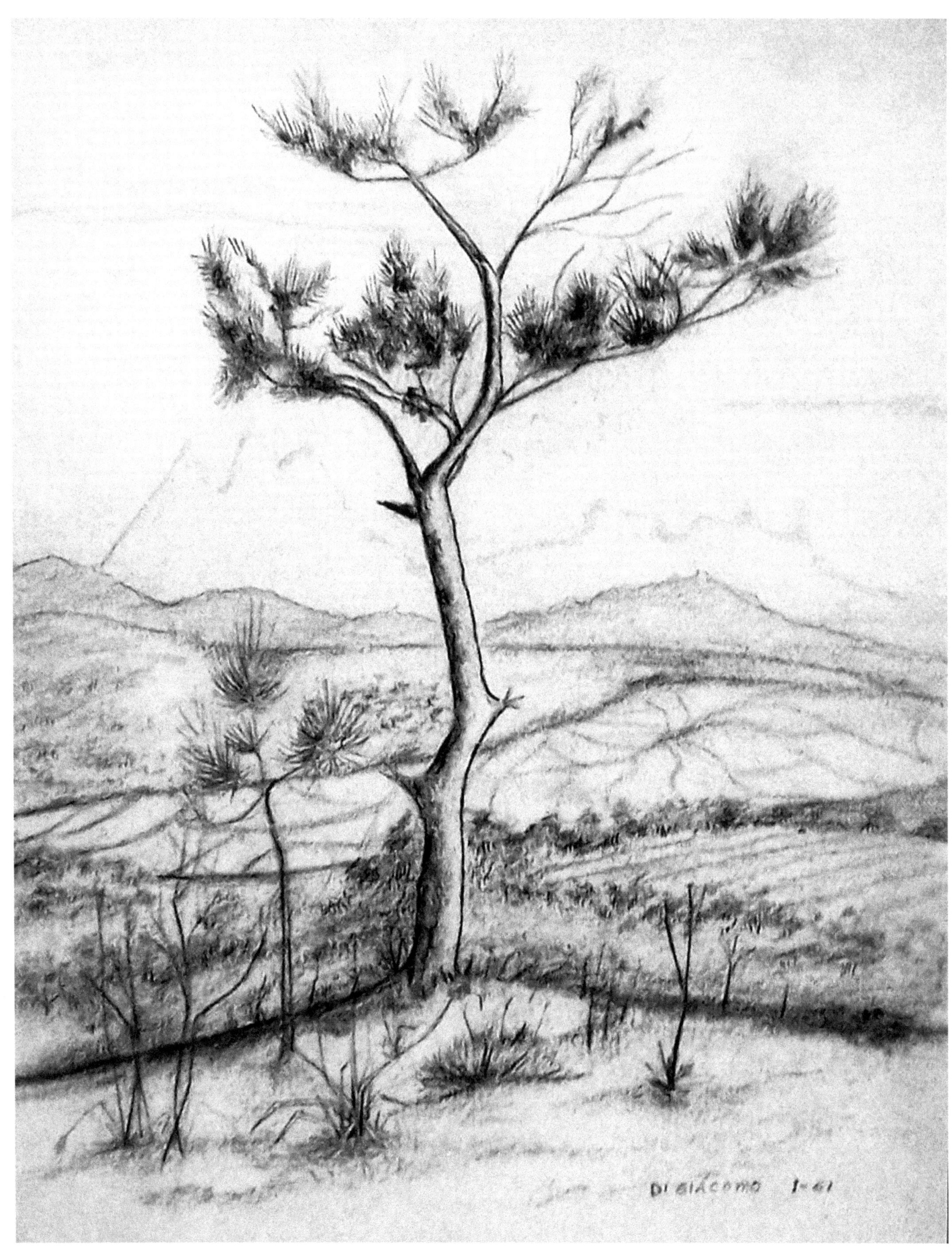

HILL 500, LOOKING OVER TO NORTH KOREA.

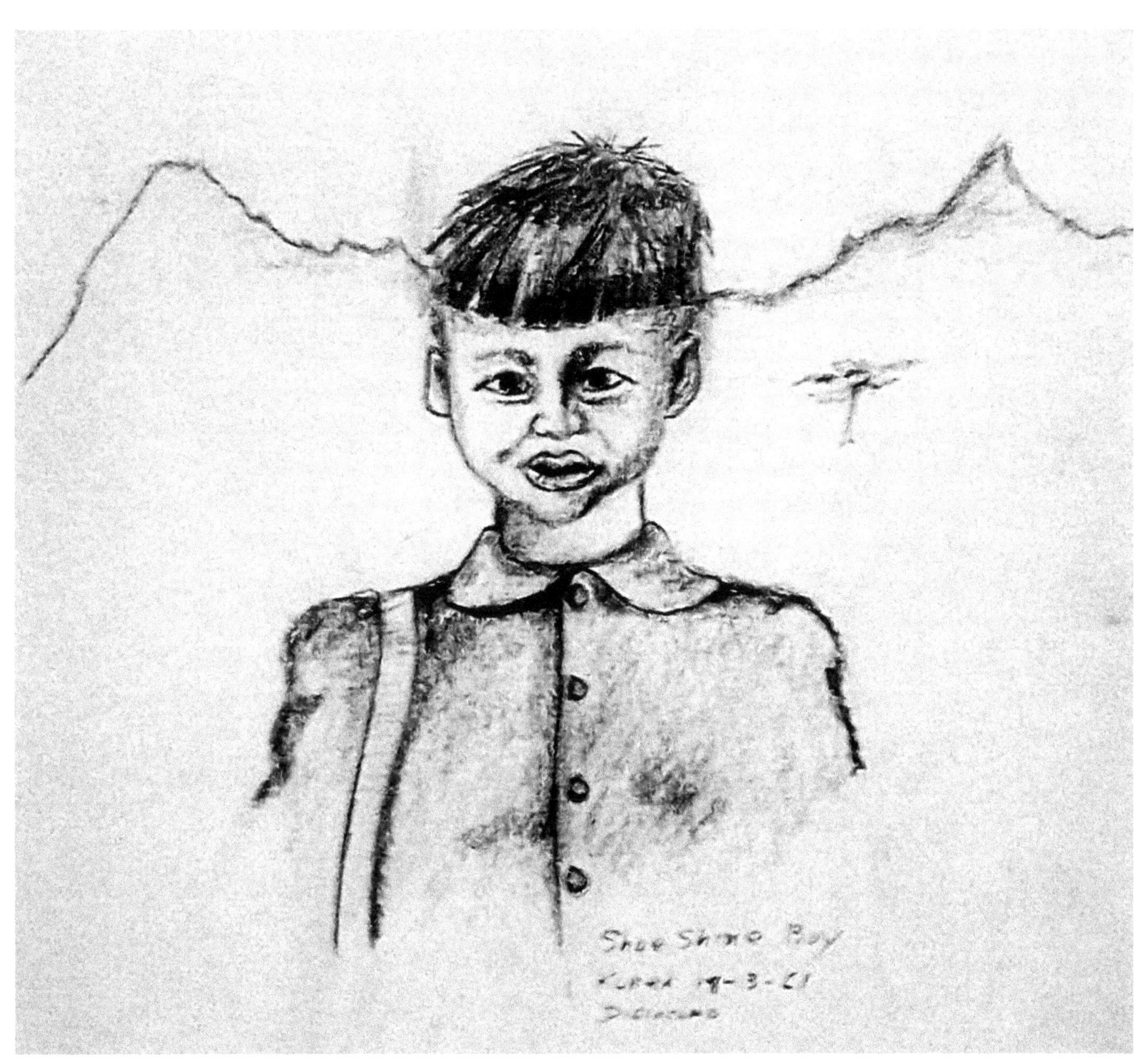

KOREAN SCHOOL BOY.

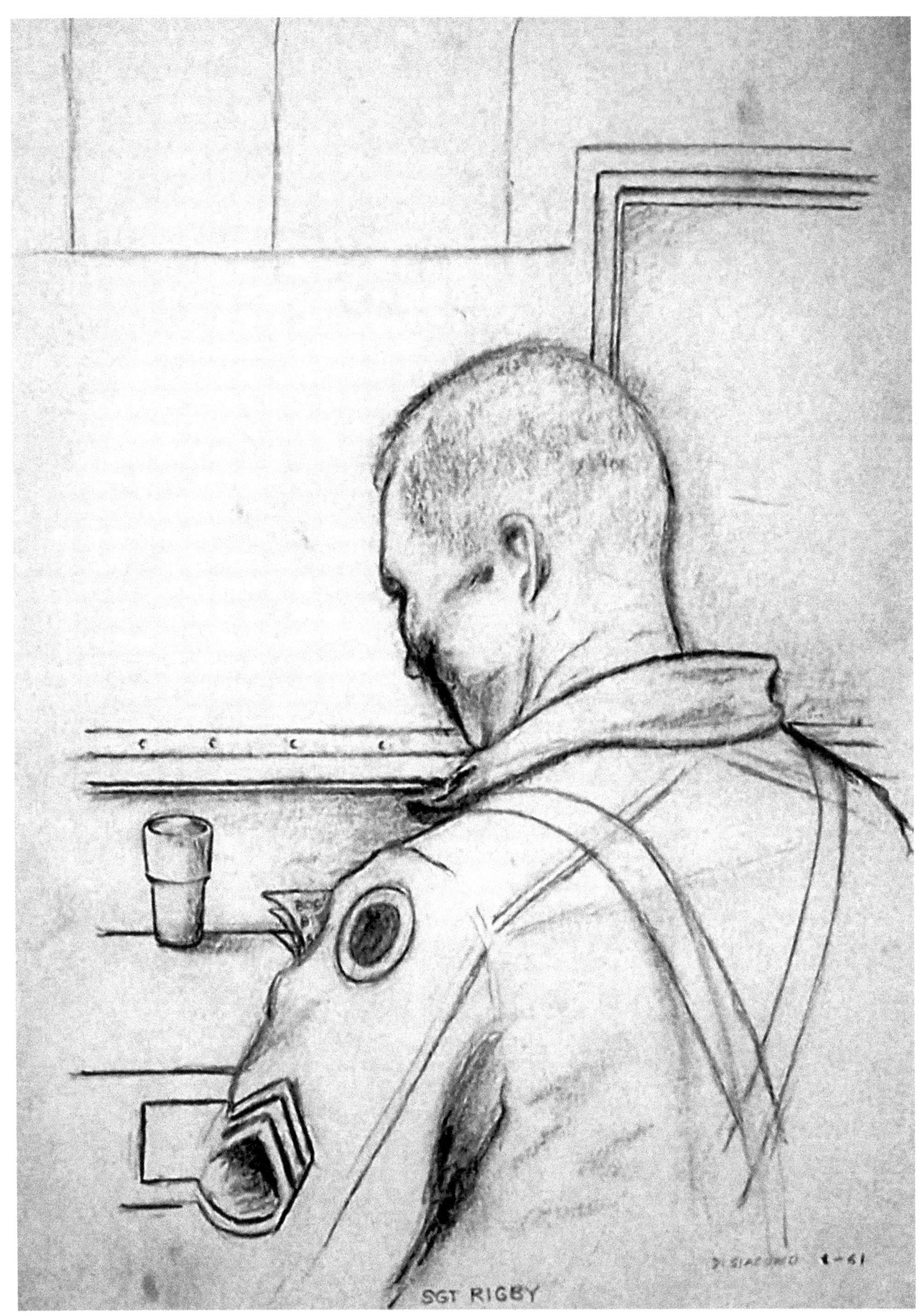

SHARGENT RIGBY

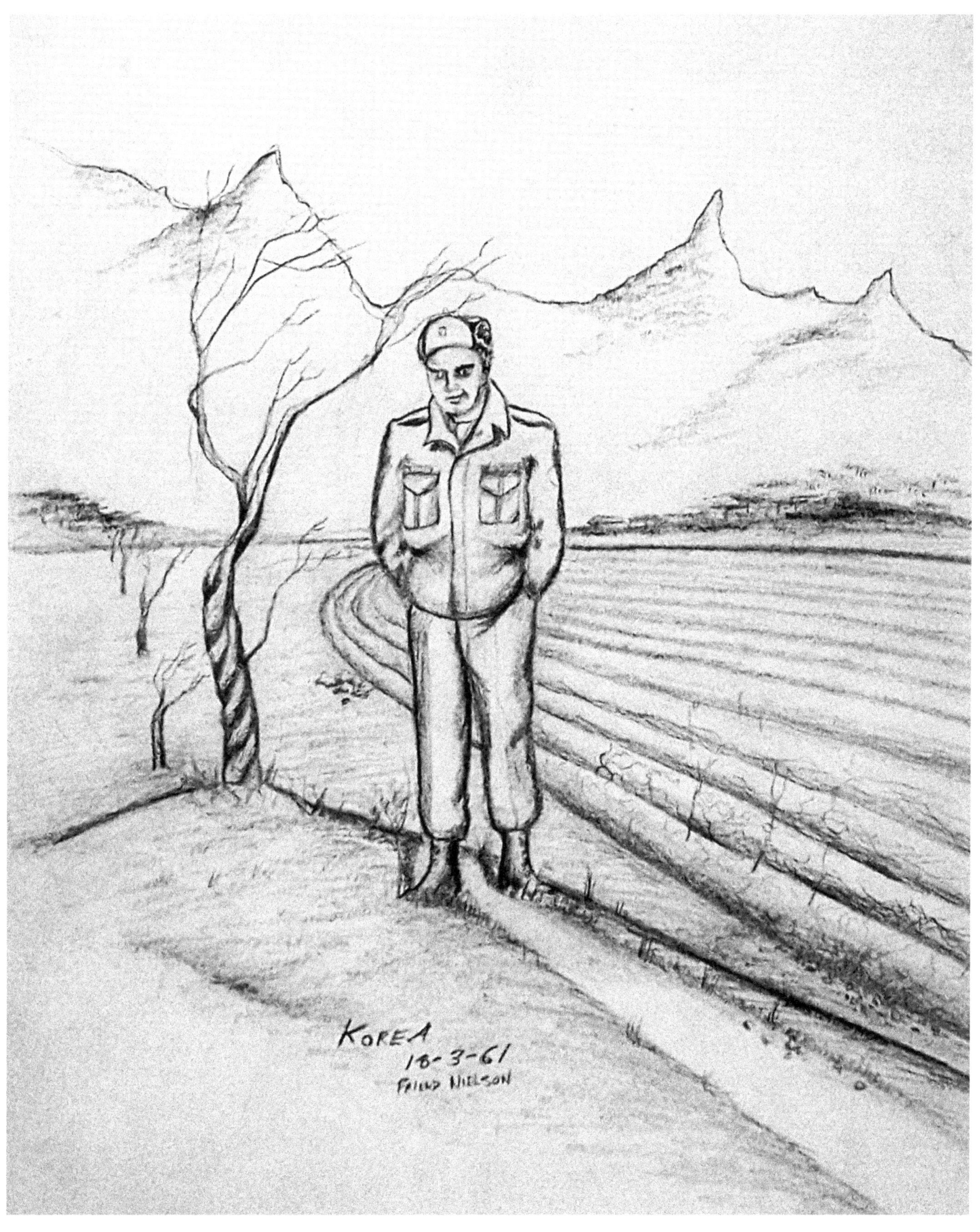

NEILSON, MY BUDDY.

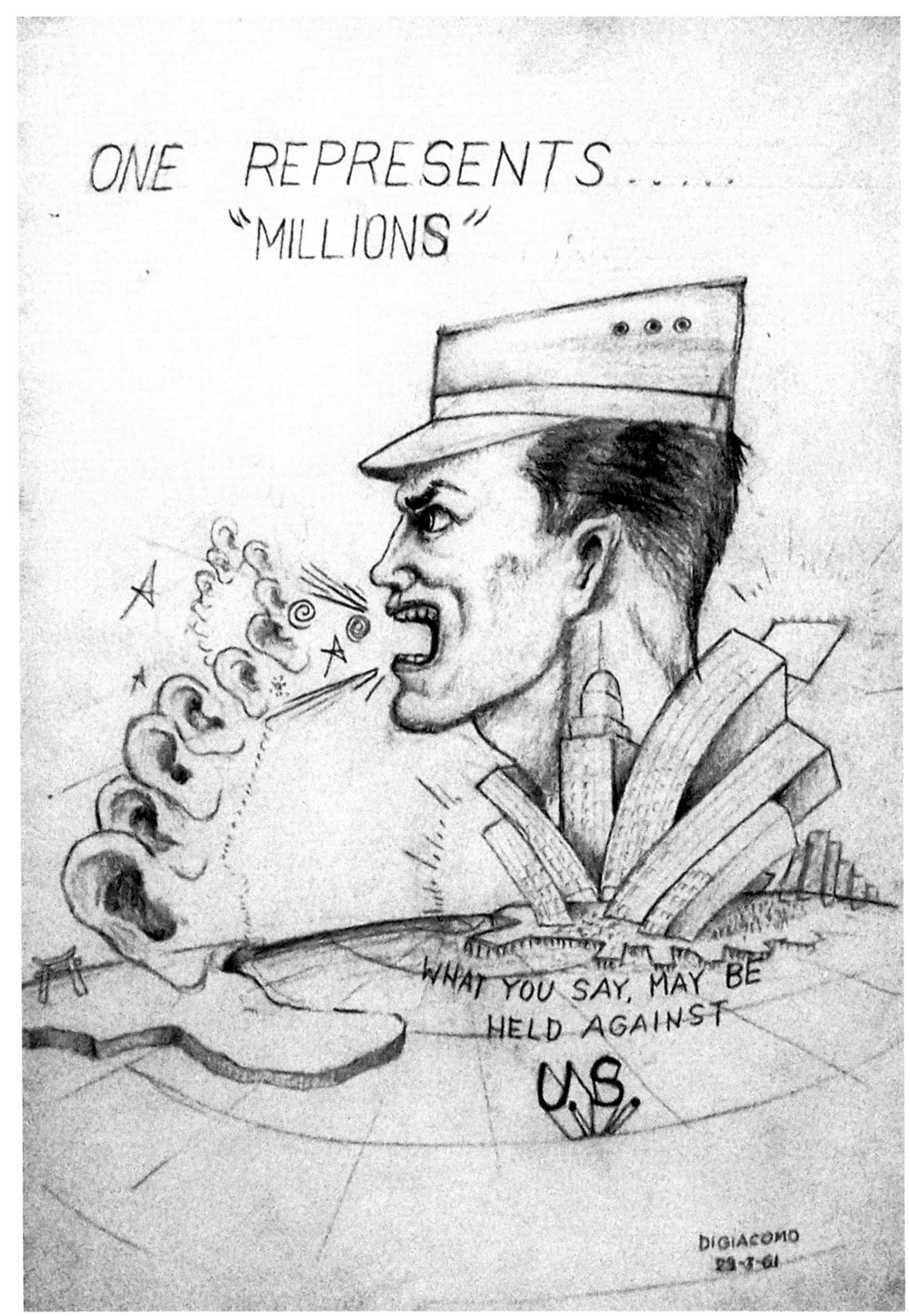

A preview of the drawing I did for the CLEAN SPEECH poster contest. I took first place in the *Stars and Stripes* newspaper in the far east.

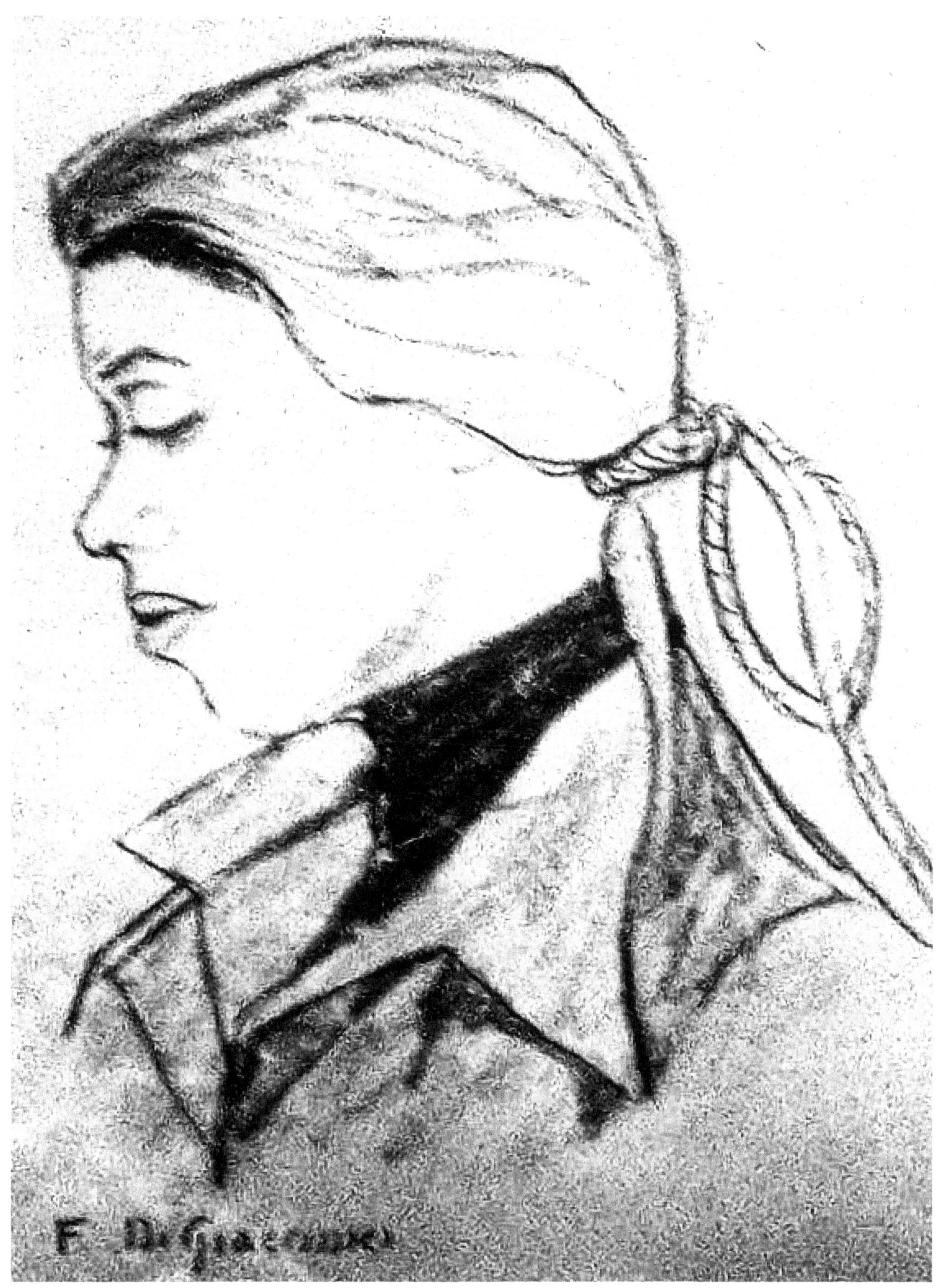

LAURA AS A YOUNG WOMAN

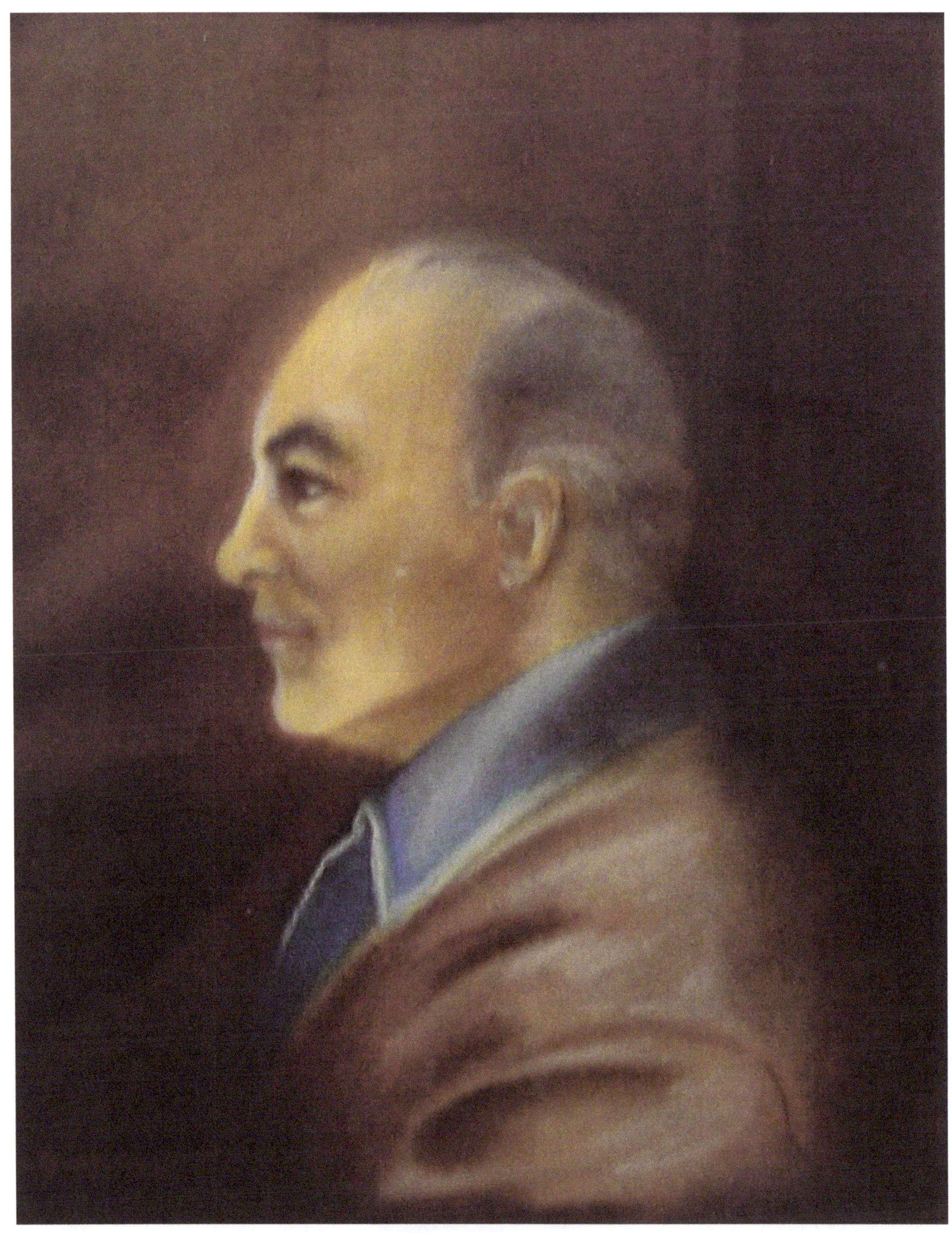

PASTEL SKETCH OF MY FATHER

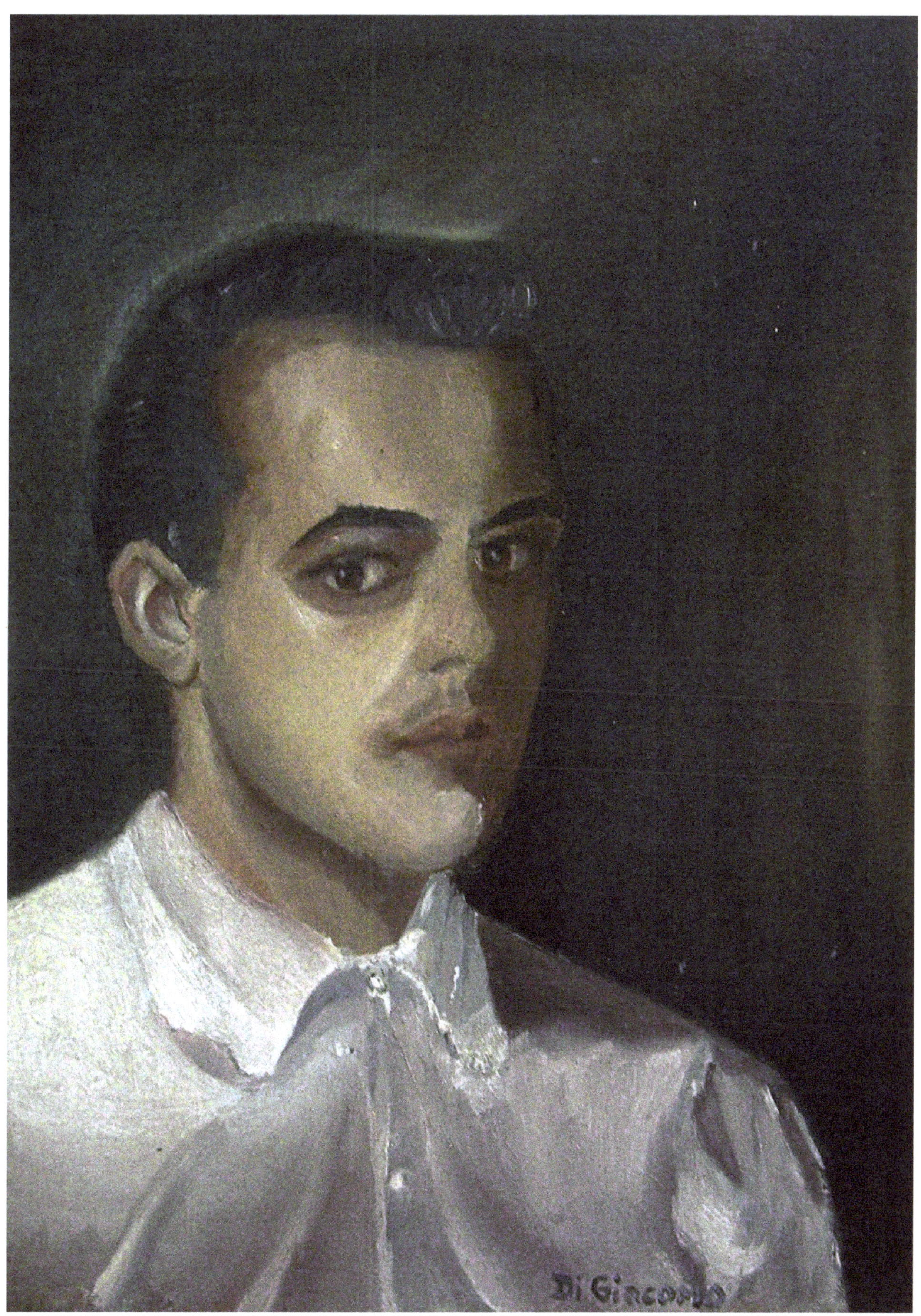

My second oil painting, a self-portrait at 20 years old

Subjects and Background at the Same Time

Paining subjects and backgrounds at the same time can be a problem. Working around the subject leaves unsightly brush strokes.

To avoid this, I make a strong outline, then paint right through leaving a slight visual of the outline. Then I take a stick from an ice cream bar and square the ends and bevel the edges. I use this to scrape the outline as shown below. This example was done with acrylic so I had to work fast. Working with oils is no problem.

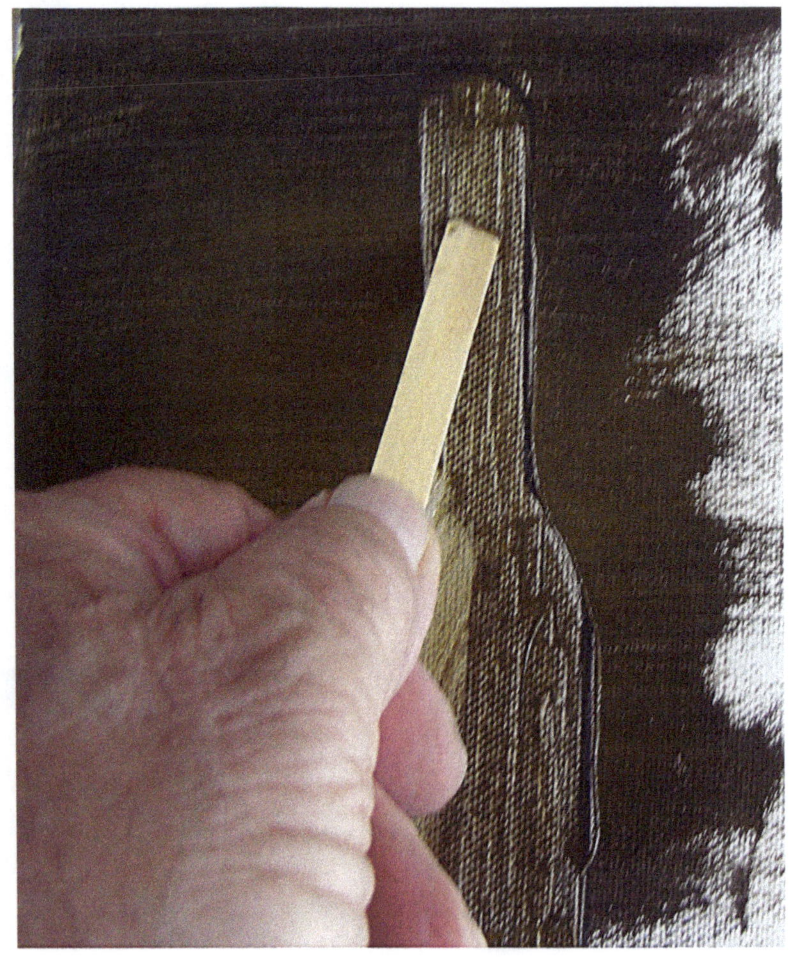

If you didn't want interference with the background, then remove most of the paint with a wet Q-tip for acrylics, and just wipe with paper towels with oils.

NOTE: Work fast with acrylic!!!

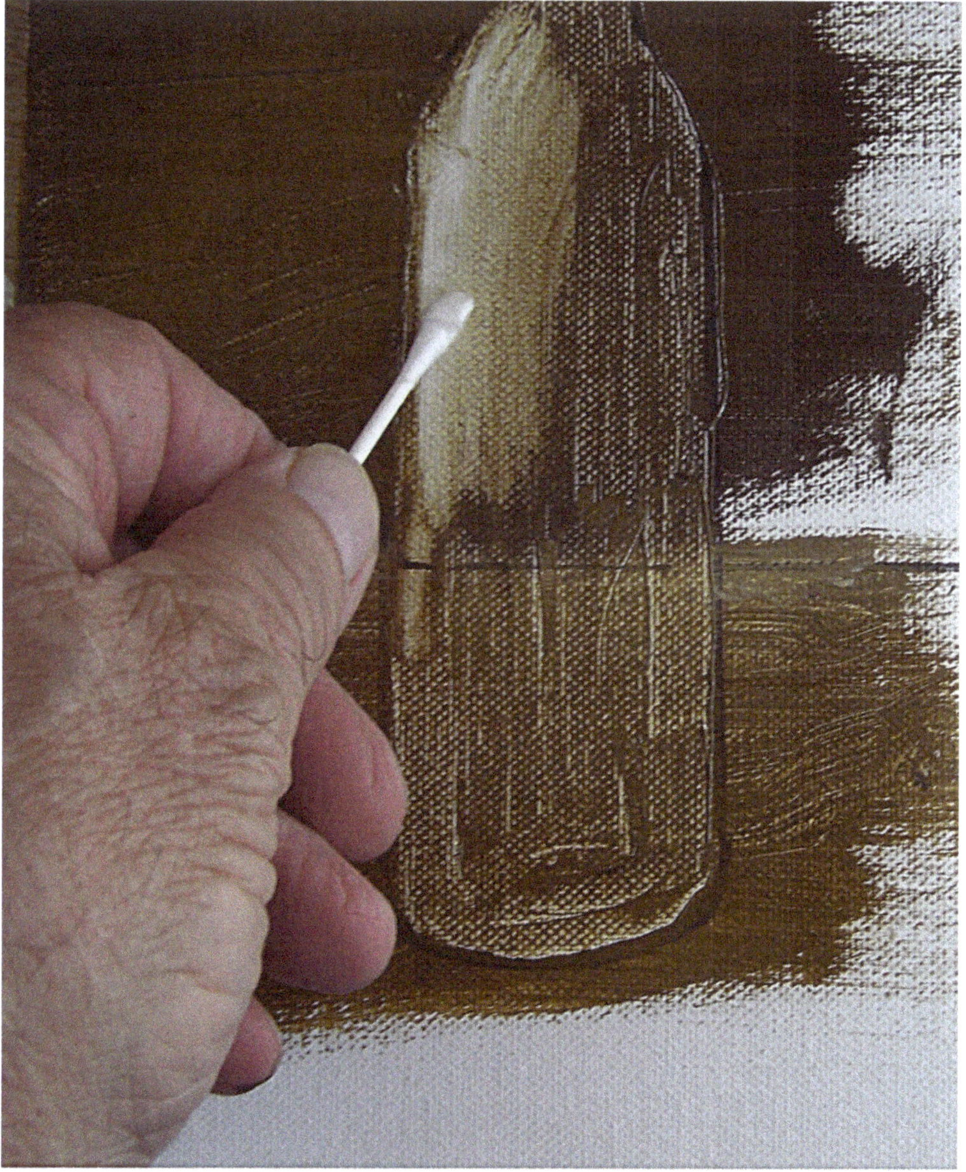

Conclusion

In conclusion, I would like to add a few notes and wish you good luck. I hope this journal has opened your eyes to a new approach to this medium.

Oh, I did forget to add that when painting the sky, keep it light — no need to tone down, and when working with fast-drying acrylic, don't use a pallet because you would be cleaning it constantly. I use Styrofoam plates.

Now remember, the best tools you can have are OBSERVATION and MEMORY. With these, you can reach your goal. I know — I'm proof.

Be sure to look for my next book dealing with POP SURREALISM.

Thank you and God Bless.